Thanks for the
article and support..
You've been great to
pan and I

Thanks
Brian

Winning
At The
Front-Line

Winning At
The Front-Line

Lessons In Creating
The Ultimate Service
Environment

Brian S. Dennis

Foto Publishing
Evanston, Illinois

This publication is designed to provide accurate and
authoritative information in regard to the subject matter
covered. It is sold with the understanding that the publisher
is not engaged in rendering legal, accounting, or other
professional service. If legal advice or other expert
assistance is required, the services of a competent
professional person should be sought.

635-5 Chicago Ave
Suite 258
Southport Plaza
Evanston, IL
60202

Printed in the U.S.A
10 9 8 7 6 5 4 3 2 1
Library of Congress Card Catalog Number: 96-85382
ISBN: 0-9653387-0-3

DENNIS'S MAXIMS

Customer: Webster defines the customer as one who purchases a commodity or service. That is not good enough! Customers are the reason your business exists. Treated properly and nurtured as one of your most valuable resources, the customer must remain your top priority.

Customer satisfaction: This is an excellent measurement of how the customer feels about your total business. This takes customer service one step further and determines if the consumer is satisfied with the entire shopping experience. Customer service is only a part of total customer satisfaction.

Customer Service: This is what I call "game time." It's how we treat those who shop our business in everyday situations. It encompasses your entire store team. How the customer is treated and building customer loyalty are important parts of this topic.

Front-liners: Those who typically work most closely with the customers. They are the eyes and ears of your business. Treat this group right if you expect to treat your customers properly. Just as in the military, this group is the most advanced and visible position within your business.

Winners: These are the businesses that have reaped the rewards of treating their customers like royalty. This book will guide you in achieving that status. Commitment and understanding customer needs are traits of this unique group. Are you ready to join them?

To: **Pamela**, my wife and best friend. You are, have
been, and will always be the love of my life.

Brian Jr., our son. Never could I realize how such
a small bundle could bring so much joy.

My Family, for making me "Do it."

CONTENTS

Preface

"It is possible to fly without motors, but not without knowledge and skill."

—Wilbur Wright

Giving great customer service fascinated me at the early age of nine. That is when my prized Bazooka bubble gum machine that was bought with the money earned from selling Christmas cards to my neighbors broke. When I went to return the defective (it really was) machine, the man at the counter began to lecture me about taking better care of my toys. Since my approach was not working, I tried the next best thing. Crying. Although not recommended past the age of nine, this last resort behavior caught the attention of the customer behind me, who demanded the owner give me a new machine.

With my head held high, I walked out of the store with a new Bazooka bubble gum machine. But something was wrong. After using all available tools to get a new machine, there was this awkward feeling in my stomach that I was not treated fairly. My goal of getting a new machine was accomplished, but I felt I did not want to spend any more of my hard earned money in this man's store.

This nine year old showed his displeasure by never buying any more candy in that store. Others may have felt the same way because the store went out of business a few years later. The day the store closed I began to question what made him go out of business and not the other store down the street that was very similar in appearance. After all, I didn't buy that much candy.

This was just one of the hundreds of experiences that were the motivation for the book. This is not a business or a how-to book. It is a book about creating the ultimate service environment before, during, and after the purchase. It is intended to be fun to read. In writing this book I constantly asked myself if this is something I would read. Or more importantly, is this material front-liners would find useful if the book was laying around on the break room table.

You will not find bar charts or complicated formulas. Instead, fresh ideas and useful information are offered that can be applied immediately. This book was fun to write and I hope you find it equally enjoyable to read.

Developing this book has afforded me the opportunity to study the art of front-line service and to interview some of the great service providers. Most of the information in this book resulted from experience rather than research. Many of the books out there on the service industry are dominated by technique-oriented concepts that are not useful in everyday practical situations. Most of what we learn in life is not learned in formal education. Rather it is the result of experiences and yes, even mistakes.

Throughout my career in the competitive retail drug industry, I have made many mistakes. For a guy who is trying to sell you a book, this may not be the most opportune time to admit this. However, as a result of those mistakes, I have learned far more than from any of my successes.

Unfortunately, the art of creating the optimal service environment does not come with an instruction book. Wouldn't it be nice if all the answers came in a box like a new toaster? Although this book makes no attempt to consider itself the ultimate instruction manual, it will provide an edge that will help you become an integral part of the success of your business.

As the manager of store development for American Drug Stores, I am afforded a unique insight into the world of service retailing and the commitment that is necessary to be the very best. American Stores Inc., our parent company, operates over 1,600 stores with 118,000 associates in twenty-six states.

Chances are you recognize some of the different names we operate under. The food operations are Jewel, Jewel/Osco, Lucky, Acme, and Super Saver. The drug stores operate under the names of Osco and Sav-on. By the time you read this, several Health 'n' Home stores will also have been opened. American Stores has outdistanced the competition for one very important reason. We have recognized the need to give the customers what they want in multiple formats and react to change quickly when their needs dictate that we do so.

When American Stores went through a reorganization effort, we did not go out and hire outside consultants. Instead we used our own people to bring the expertise and knowledge of how it's done now and what steps need to be taken. This book reflects that mission statement by using the many ideas received from the front-liners I worked with on a daily basis.

What you will read is not a strategy or a philosophy. Rather it is a common sense approach to giving that extra level of service and keeping the customer coming back and back and back. That means making the job fun! It also warrants mastering the art of listening. To this day I still have not learned anything while my mouth was open. It is not a come to work – do the job –and check your brain at the time clock approach.

After you read each paragraph, I want you to feel the passion and dedication needed to be the best. It has been my goal to share the understanding of results that great customer satisfaction can bring to an organization that is willing to be customer driven. Not customer focused.

This book is unlike any you may have read in the past. The information is provided in an easy to read manner and lets the reader step into the shoes of a front-liner. We all had that one teacher who could make any subject enjoyable no matter how uninteresting the material. Such teachers do not just recite information from the text. Instead, they surround the information with related examples and present it in an easy to understand format.

For every lesson you learn in this book, there is a real life story to go with it. This makes the lessons applicable and therefore encourages you to relate them to your own experiences. As you journey through the book with me, there will be times when your blood pressure will boil as you associate with some of the more frustrating service experiences you may have had.

The chapters in the book were designed to be short but packed with useful information. Think of it as an all you can eat buffet. You want to sample a small portion of all the different items the buffet has to offer. In this book, you won't load your plate up with only two or three ideas. Rather, I offer many ideas in digestible, bite size pieces.

Each page will take you through the steps necessary to be a service winner where it counts. At the front-line. The topics are numerous but they all add up to a complete and comprehensive look at total front-line commitment.

As you absorb the material ask yourself, what am I going to do differently today that I did not do yesterday? Managers, challenge yourself and the employees to better impact your service environment with each turn of the page. Front-liners, use the concepts discussed in the following chapters and you will begin to see the results that giving great service can bring.

Well, what are we waiting for? LET'S GO!

One
Know
Thy Customer

"Whatever is flexible and blowing will continue to grow, what ever is rigid and blocked will whither and die."

–Tho Te Ching

By now, organizations have learned that one of the most important assets of a company is its customers.

Managing this valuable commodity requires dissecting the characteristics that make up your customer. Although this may require added time and resources, the benefits can be enormous. Let me give you some examples.

Banc One of Columbus, Ohio, analyzed its customer base and discovered some amazing results. It found twenty percent of its customers provided the bank's entire profit while the remaining eighty percent actually cost the bank money. By identifying this portfolio of information, Bank One is better able to serve this group with added benefits and rewards.

Mercer Management Consulting concluded up to 80 percent of cellular phone revenues comes from 20 to 25 percent of cellular customers. Once this group is identified, then the cellular companies will be better able to serve them.

Of the numerous reports, business journals and trade magazines I researched for this book, many showed statistics that were amazingly consistent. Try and digest these numbers.

Why Customers Leave

14 percent leave because complaints are not solved

9 percent leave because of the competition

9 percent leave because they move

68 percent leave for no special reason

Incredible! Almost seven out of ten customers who spent money in your store and who are no longer doing business with you cannot explain why. Were they not treated as special or greeted upon entering your business? Or maybe they felt your organization did not recognize their needs.

Knowing who is shopping at your stores and restaurants can give you an enormous advantage over your closest competitor. Let's look at that 68 percent who leave for no special reason.

If your organization can target and react to this customer base, then you stand a greater chance of keeping them. This 68 percent is yours for the taking. Deliver the type of service I speak about in this book and watch that number drop.

Companies today are constantly compiling huge amounts of database information on the customers who shop in their stores. Through the rapid use of preferred cards, VIP cards and numerous other information seeking tools, these businesses know their customers better than ever before. Separating and understanding the complex components that are accumulated through this data remains the challenge.

Still, the most accurate means of finding out who your customers are and determining their needs is as simple as asking and listening. Mastering this technique requires getting close to your customers.

Delta Air Lines conducts weekly telephone interviews with its frequent flyers. The information is readily used to better provide the programs and services their customers are asking for.

The first-class lunch and dinner menus the past winter were determined by those flyers who use that service the most. Delta invited more than 100 SkyMiles™ members to participate in a taste testing session for their North American regional cuisine. The final decisions were based on the feedback from the SkyMiles™ participants.

Delta also became a smoke-free airline based on the surveys of 26,000 Delta customers. Delta Air Lines Chairman, President, and Chief Executive Officer Ronald W. Allen describes Delta's commitment to the customers it serves.

"We are listening to you now more than ever before, and we plan to increase our efforts in the future. We believe the results from listening will provide the service you want and expect from Delta. That is our goal as a recognized customer service leader in the airline industry."

I am a SkyMiles participant with Delta and can attest to their commitment to be the best. Listening to their customers and giving them what they want gives this company an advantage over many of the other airlines I have flown.

Know thy customer has been a retail maxim for years. Today it is even more important to understand the complex target consumer as the complexion of this group changes. What may have been your customer make-up five years ago, might not be so today, let alone in years to come. The consumers in the United States are changing and at a rapid pace.

The U.S Bureau of the Census shows by the year 2050, whites will comprise only 53 percent of the nation's consumers, a dramatic drop from the 1990s' 76 percent. What will the other 47 percent be? Some 88 million will be of Hispanic origin; 56 million will be African-American; and 38 million will be of Asian and Pacific Islander origin.

The most rapidly growing ethnic group is Hispanics. By 2010, this group is projected to be the second largest in the United States. That means today they represent one in ten Americans; by the year 2050 they will represent one in five.

Reaching this new customer base poses many problems for those who do not recognize these growing categories of shoppers. It will become increasingly challenging as minority Americans maintain their languages and cultures rather than assimilating into the mainstream. For example, 50 percent of all Hispanics speak Spanish exclusively.

If a business wants to survive in the future, it needs to understand these new consumers and the goods and services they will demand to satisfy their needs. The story goes that one store had a single sign posted in Spanish and that read, "Shoplifters will be prosecuted to the fullest extent of the law." If I were a Hispanic shopper, that would probably be my last visit to that store.

Understanding the needs of a changing customer base means better appreciating what this customer wants. They will reward those who cater to their needs and as this group increases every year, your business has the opportunity to grow with them.

Knowing the customers who shop your business means constantly finding out who they are. Stay close to this group. Realize the make-up of this group is constantly changing and your business must adapt to the needs of the customer. Giving consumers reasons to shop your stores requires knowing who they are and what they want. It is easy. Just listen.

- **Recognize who your customers are and deliver what they want.**
- **Know the characteristics that makeup your customer.**
- **Give the customers reasons to shop at your store. Let them know you truly care about them.**

Two

Serving the Internal Customer

"If opportunity doesn't knock ... build a door."

—Milton Berle

Jan Carlzon who led the incredible turnaround of, Scandinavian Airlines Systems, described it best when he said "If you are not serving the customer, your job is to be serving someone who is." We all know who our external customers are, but are we also recognizing the internal customers of our organization?

This book is the result of many people. However, one person has truly impacted how I treat the internal customers of our business. That individual is Donna Pfeifer. Donna has left this world after a long bout with cancer but will be missed forever. If you were a district manager, regional vice-president, store manager, or any other person who came into contact with Donna, you will agree with me that she was by far the best at providing internal customer service.

When I was a store set-up coordinator, Donna was the secretary in charge of all my projects. You see, she always took the new coordinators under her wing when they came to work in her department. Our boss did not strike as much fear in us as Donna did with her impeccable standards that each of us would have to maintain on a daily basis.

She could have been confused with a drill sergeant in the army had you not gotten to know her. Promptness, good grooming standards, and a commitment to be the best was all instilled in us by Donna.

I do not think she ever met one of the thousands of customers who benefited from her behind the scenes magic. The coordinator for the project, was to funnel all problems and complications of opening a new store back through Donna, who in turn would call the necessary people to correct them.

Many of the problems would require almost investigative-type work to resolve them in time for the store's grand opening. Chopping through all the different layers to get the problem corrected was an art and Donna was the artist. She knew the set-up coordinator, district manager and more importantly, the customer, all counted on her to fix the problems.

We were her customers and nothing would stand in the way of satisfying us. When vendors told us that merchandise racks would not arrive in time for grand opening, Donna got them there. Consistently, she amazed us with her service-first attitude. Although she never came in direct contact with our external customers, Donna always knew that providing to the internal customers was the next best thing.

How many times have you been frustrated by your own organization when you were unable to get a particular service or need rendered properly? Understanding that great service is needed in each layer of the business and not just the ones touching the external customer directly is the challenge many of us face. We can accomplish this role by identifying those who are the internal customers of our business.

Whether you are a buyer, human resource manager, systems specialist, administrative assistant or perform another task that involves working in an organization, you will impact others within on a regular basis. How the information is handled between different departments and layers of structure will be a contributing factor to how the external customers are also being served.

The saying goes, "Never give a first class carpenter second class tools." That applies to your business as well. If you are striving to give great service in the stores and organizations you work in, then the support facilities should also pledge to deliver this kind of service behind the scenes. Giving your business the best possible package the support facilities can offer requires the internal employees to render a service package that is equally committed.

When I was a store manager calling the office with a question or concern, on a rare occasion, the service received was less than poor. It seemed a few of the employees were not much concerned about delivering service to the store teams. Instead when a store phoned in, it was viewed as a nuisance rather than an opportunity to solve a problem. From the store side, this leaves you with the impression that the office does not have the same goals and commitments as you do.

Now these instances only involved a few of the hundreds of employees who worked at the corporate office; most provided the stores with quick responses and a caring approach. How they interact with each other as internal customers will affect all within the organization; that is both internal and external customers.

Since coming into the corporate office for American Drug Stores, I have had the opportunity to work with some of the best service providers within our organization. It does not matter to these individuals what department or group is requesting the information. They provide it accurately and within a very short time. Watching how they treat others within and the attitude on the importance of delivering great service are all traits of these service providers. Although they never see the customers our stores serve every day, they do understand the importance of their job role and how it ultimately has an impact on the customer directly.

This author recommends that all corporate offices and support facilities take an annual reality check. Let the staff spend a day or even a week in the store, restaurants, or service-oriented business that you operate in. This will immediately give them a much better understanding of what it takes to be a winner in today's competitive arena. I guarantee after a week, if they were not providing optimal service to the internal customers of your business before, they will be now.

Identifying the internal customers of your business is a matter of recognizing the people who come in contact with you in the organization. By taking a service first approach with them, you too can be a major contributor in the success of the business you operate in.

If I could put Donna's internal service attitude in a jar and give each of you a small sample of what it included, I

would. Obviously this is not possible, so at best I can only carry on the torch of her message. For somewhere high above, I am sure the angels are giving better service now. Donna would not have it any other way.

- **Internal customer service impacts external service.**
- **Identify the internal customers and let them know they are important to you.**
- **Allow office and support facilities to meet your external customers.**

Three

Front-liners: Making the Difference

"We have met the enemy and he is us."

–Pogo

Y ou know who they are. The hundreds of employees who come in contact with you each week. They fill the roles of clerks, salespersons, cashiers, cooks, and many other job titles that perform a service function. They are the bread and butter of your business and have the ability to make a major impact upon one of your most important assets, the customer.

Typically they come in contact more often with the customers than do the other positions that manage them. Each day brings new challenges and opportunities to win customers. Your business is the battle and these employees are the front-liners.

If treated properly and given the tools to succeed, these front-liners represent the best possible view of your business to the customer. They are the window to the goods and services that make up the business. Front-liners are also the eyes and ears of the business. If you want to know what the customer thinks of your organization, then you better ask the ones who work most closely with the customer each day.

No, these are not just employees. The front-liners carry a far greater level of importance than any other area of your business. For if they are not delivering the message described in this book every day, then the organization has very little opportunity of serving the customer properly. If the customer is not served properly, then chances are the business will not be around very long.

I have seen front-liners who play the customers like a well-tuned piano. I have also seen front-liners who literally fought and disagreed with customers arguing their point. What separates these two groups? What makes one front-liner leave me smiling while another has really made me mad?

There are numerous answers but it all starts with giving front-liners what they need to excel at their job task. If you want front-liners to deliver great service at the donut counter, then make sure you have plenty of donuts, a register that works, adequate help, and the ability to make the customer happy. It does not have to be a state of the art facility, but it does need to offer the front-liners a working environment that lets them perform their magic.

I always put the front-liners ahead of the customers at the stores I managed. My philosophy is that if I am not treating this group properly, how can I expect them to treat the customers right? If they had children, school, football practice or any other responsibility, the management team was instructed to work around their schedules as best as the business needs would allow. Out of the hundreds of employees I had the honor to manage, only a few tried to take advantage of this opportunity. The remaining vast majority saw it as a privilege.

Front-liners do not come to work to intentionally do a bad job. In fact studies show that most front-liners enjoy their jobs if they are allowed to satisfy the customer's needs. Most front-liners enjoy the satisfaction of a job well done. If they provide great service and are able to witness the visible results that come from it, then the front-liners will foster a service-oriented business daily.

The importance of front-line employees will be apparent as you read through the chapters. Just as a plant needs to be watered to keep growing, so do your employees. If allowed to satisfy the customer, they will grow along with the business. However, if forgotten, the front-liner's and organization's service skills, will wilt.

I have had the opportunity and good fortune to work with some of the best service employees out there today. To you I say thank you. When you read this book, give yourself a pat on the back because you deserve it. Not only did you make my job an exciting one, but you showed me how a team can have fun winning the service game.

By the end of this book, I believe you will have a greater respect and reverence for the front-liners who help your business run. If in the past you have viewed them only as part-time cashiers or clerks, you will soon understand the important role they play. Tapping into the potential that exists within this group of employees is the first step in identifying the opportunities that will be afforded to the organization.

This is an open letter to Leonard Stern, the owner of Hartz Mountain Corporation that was placed in the November 28, 1995, *Wall Street Journal.*.

As a recently retired employee of Hartz Mountain I want to express my thanks and gratitude to you. During my 22 years with the company I have witnessed your personal involvement in matters inside and outside the realm of business. I have grown to appreciate your caring acts of kindness to myself and others. In my experience your concern for people is unparalleled in the business world.

I see evidence of your caring attitude in each and every Hartz Mountain product. I only wish more pet owners knew you and your company the way I do.

Jim O'Gorman

Wow! A front-liner who took the time and expense to say thank you to a leader who he felt treated his employees and customers a little bit differently. I bet Jim O'Gorman treated others in a similar manner. When this kind of caring attitude is prevalent and operating at the top of the business, then it becomes very easy for others to take this torch of service and run with it.

At the drug store I managed, the front-liners would challenge themselves to solve as many customer concerns that were brought to their attention. Very seldom would they call for my assistance. It was important to each of them that a customer concern could be handled at the cashier or stock clerk level. They realized the management team did not look at them as just position fillers. Rather they saw themselves as problem-solvers, greeters, sales floor managers and as many of the other jobs they performed.

This group of front-liners was a proactive team of winners who cared about the job they did as well as the satisfaction that came with it. Your team has the opportunity to provide your organization with similar results if the power of these front-liners is realized and nurtured. The sky is the limit, so let them fly.

- **Front-liners are the pulse of your service program.**
- **Coaching the front-liners to succeed is a continual process.**
- **Given the right stage to perform on, the front-liners will discover the inner potential for pleasing the customer.**

Four

Nuts and Bolts: Winning the Frontcounter™

"The speed of the leader is the speed of the pack."

—Yukon Proverb

One of the most important areas of customer satisfaction is the interaction between the employee and the customer. These interactions can take place thousands of times every day in your business. Of the many organizations I visit each year, most make a modest attempt to satisfy the customer or at a minimum at least acknowledge their presence. For many stores out there, this is their version of customer interaction.

I coined the phrase Frontcounters™. This represents the interaction that takes place when a customer and a **front-liner encounter** each other in your place of business. These Frontcounters™ can happen anywhere. In the cosmetic aisle, the drive-through at McDonald's, the lobby at your favorite hair salon, or wherever the customer comes into contact with the front-liners. Today's businesses must be trained and staffed to properly handle these meetings.

Recently, I was touring some of our stores in the Boston, Massachusetts, area. We were following a set itinerary that listed all the stores to be visited during our trip. While driving, I noticed that we passed a store that was not on our list but was due to be remodeled the following year. I asked that we stop and take a quick look around the store to better understand some of the remodeling concerns that the store manager might have.

After pulling into the parking lot, we had a Frontcounter™ with a front-liner who was gathering carts. He welcomed us to the store and told us we needed a cart to carry out the great savings that were inside the store. He did not know that we were from the corporate office nor did he suspect we were evaluating the store for the future remodel. Yet, he had us feeling great about the store and we were still in the parking lot!

No less than three more positive Frontcounters™ took place before even getting to the service desk. These front-liners did not wait until we got to the checkout to deliver great service. They were providing it as we went throughout the store. This was one of our most profitable stores in the eastern region and it was easy to see why.

A Frontcounter™ can be as simple as a "Hello" or "Can I help you pick out some coffee." Later in the book, we will examine opportunities in acknowledging the customer. In this lesson, I am more interested with communicating the importance of Frontcounters™ both for the front-liner and the customer.

While my wife and I were vacationing in Italy, we stopped in a small town called Sorrento. This town is

famous for its inlaid wood art work. This painstaking process requires an artist to combine thousands of small pieces of wood to form a picture.

These pieces come in many shapes and sizes and you could fit a hundred of them on your fingernail alone. As individual wood pieces they have very little shape or form. However, as they combine all these tiny pieces together, a beautiful work of art is soon formed. If standing a few feet away, you are unable to tell this incredible work of art is made from such minute pieces of wood.

Frontcounters™ are very similar to this ancient art form. The individual meetings the customers and employees have may not seem very important at the time. But, when a customer begins combining these Frontcounters™, they begin to see a much larger picture of quality service. This is similar to a boxing match. It is not always the knockout punch that wins the fight but the hundreds of others that preceded it.

If you ever want to see the art of Frontcounters™ in action and you are fortunate enough to have The Home Depot in your area, go visit it soon. Home Depot is the largest home improvement warehouse in the country with over 400 stores and sales topping 12 billion. It is not possible to walk down an aisle in this mega size super store without having at least one Frontcounter™. The staff not only greets you in a friendly manner but will offer you assistance on where to find that special tool or part you need.

If the front-liners do not know where to find something or they are not experts in a particular area of the store, you can bet they will go out of their way until they can find the right person who can help you. The employees at Home

Depot have an attitude that each and every Frontcounter™ is important.

Americans today spend billions of dollars each year fixing up their homes themselves. Not all of these do-it-yourselfers are professionals; many require individualized service they can relate to. The Home Depot has catered to this group of customers. After identifying this niche in the market, they set out to make sure that every customer who comes into their store will experience several positive Frontcounters™ before they leave.

On my last visit to the store, I counted thirteen front-liners who asked me if I needed help. This company is not waiting until you get to the checkout before they give great service. They are providing it every day, in every aisle, to every customer.

As a result of this superior service, Fortune magazine named Home Depot their most admired retailer in a survey of over 400 corporations in 40 industries.

If you think about all the Frontcounters™ that you are involved in every day, how many can you remember recently that really made an impact on your future purchasing decisions? It should be our goal to ensure that the customer walks away from each Frontcounter™ with a better feeling than before they met you.

My goal as a manager was to truly delight the first customer who walked into the store each morning, thus setting the tone for the remainder of the day for the front-liners to encourage positive Frontcounters™. When front-liners see their leaders providing great service, it begins to form habits among the crew that will last for a long, long time.

These Frontcounters™ and how to manage them will be one of the hottest topics in the business world in years to come. Those organizations that are committed to providing the ultimate service environment will surely want this weapon in their arsenal. Mastering these encounters will allow businesses to "wow" customers and build a lasting loyalty.

When I was little, there was nothing better than waking up on Saturday morning and jumping in the family station wagon to go to the grocery store with my mother. After all, somebody had to make sure she bought the cereal with the most sugar in it. Anyway, when we finished gathering all the groceries for a family of eight, my mom would always head to Michelle's checkout. Even if others were less crowded, we always looked forward to Michelle ringing us out. Were we abnormal or without anything better to do on a Saturday morning? I think not!

We enjoyed the weekly Frontcounter™ that Michelle provided. My mother chatted with her as she rang up the groceries and I just gloated as she told me how big and strong I was getting. Occasionally she would have extra coupons for my mother and a hidden piece of bubble gum for me. These Frontcounters™ kept us going back to that store week after week.

Every business needs a few Michelles. They are the ones who truly differentiate themselves from others and make all their Frontcounters™ great ones. Going through the motions will not cut it. Memorable Frontcounters™ need to be genuine and sincere.

Customers do business every day with front-liners who recite a standard greeting with little or no emotion. For some it is an effort to pick up their heads and greet you. Do not fall into this trap. Show the front-liners these Frontcounters™ can be fun and are certainly an important part of their role. Encourage this behavior and reward those who do it well.

One does not need a forty-piece band for each Frontcounter™, but some individual emotion and sincerity will go a long way toward exciting the customer. Many consumers do not have high expectations because of the dismal service they have received in the past. Therefore it may not take more than a few extraordinary Frontcounters™ to win their initial business and a consistency of many more to keep them coming back.

- **Make each Frontcounter™ a rewarding one.**
- **Frontcounters™ allow you to deliver great service before the customer expects it.**
- **Good Frontcounters™ are contagious. Have fun with them and so will the customers.**

Five

Hello and Thank You.
Now was that
Hard to Say?

"He who stops being better stops being good."

–Oliver Cromwell

Sometimes it is the simple things in life that keep us happy. A "Thank you" or "Have a nice day" when you have finished paying for your purchase. Yes, a simple gesture but all too often a forgotten one.

Coming back from visiting some our Milwaukee, Wisconsin, stores, I asked the group to stop at a huge discount mall on the way home to get some new ideas for some merchandising fixtures. As we pulled in, I asked them to count the number of people who work in the different stores who say hello to us. Then, I asked the same group to count the number of employees at the different stores that I said hello to first.

Reluctantly they agreed to play along. The first stop was a very large department store. The score after leaving there was Brian 10 hellos/department store employees 0.

The next stop was a book store. This time a little bit better. Brian 3/ employees 1. Continuing on, we stopped at a discount clothing store. You guessed it, Brian 6/ employees 0.

Doing simple math after three stores, I said hello to 19 front-liners while they in turn recognized me only once. I asked the others what was difficult about saying hello to customers as they entered each of the different departments. None of the employees seemed to be performing any functions that would not allow them to be able to acknowledge our presence with a greeting.

Am I making a big deal out of a simple hello or welcome? I do not think so. Not only does the customer feel ignored if not acknowledged but will avoid your store in the future if he or she is made to feel unwelcome.

Most customers would much rather do their shopping in a store that recognizes and greets them with a sincere hello. Made to feel more comfortable in this type of store setting, the customer will prefer to do additional business with you in the future.

Do you identify with those stores that know who you are and really appreciate your business? Although only a handful of businesses and consumers have this type of relationship, the ones that do will often not let you leave the store without a sincere thank you. These operators know that loyal customers are difficult to find and the simple acts of gratitude should not be taken for granted.

Wal-Mart has spent millions of dollars on its greeting program. What a novel concept of having somebody stand by the door and say hello to the customers as they enter the store. They have developed an image of friendliness that is far superior to that of any other business operating out there today. When you enter the store, not only are you greeted with a friendly hello, but will get immediate assistance with aisle directions, a wheelchair, or any other amenity to make your shopping experience more enjoyable.

Saying hello to each and every customer should be the responsibility of all front-liners. Businesses can learn from the Wal-Marts of the world that customers demand recognition. If you treat all your customers in this manner, you may be surprised at the results.

Saying thank you seems to be another obstacle in the service industry. I am not sure why, but these seem to be the two hardest words in the dictionary to say. Most of us were taught at an early age to say thank you when we received a present or a piece of candy from the barber. Because this seems to be a recently lost art form, it may require some training to jump start this much needed reply from front-liners.

What? Training the front-liners to say something as simple as a thank you? I am not kidding. That is what the Delaware River Port Authority did. Not long ago they announced their "Thank You, Every Toll, Every Time" program.

Officials of this organization announced to the press that 175 toll collectors had been trained to say "thank you" as they collected a toll. A simple thanks would not do. Although some may question if it is worth the time and, tollpayers' expense to conduct a training program to say thank you, I think it is very important. We toll road users appreciate this seldom heard response.

A simple thank you is quite possibly the last Frontcounter™ you may have with the customer. You worked very hard to make his or her shopping experience a memorable one. Do not let the customer walk out that door without saying "Thanks" or "We really appreciate your business." You might say it's the cherry on the sundae. Oh. And by the way. Thank you for reading this.

- Say hello to every customer/ every time.
- Say thank you to all your customers.
- Say hello to every customer/ every time.
- Say thank you to all your customers.

Six

Oh No!
That Place is Awful

"So much of what we call management consists of making it difficult for people to work."

−Peter Drucker

When my wife and I moved into our new home, we decided that some of the thirteen foot windows would require blinds. After shopping a few stores, we decided to go with a local company in Chicago. When we chose the style of blinds that we wanted, they promised proper installation and quick service at an agreed upon price. This was encouraging information and Pam and I left feeling confident about our purchase.

Unfortunately, they failed at every Frontcounter™ after we left the store. When the bill came, it was wrong. When the installer came, he did not have the proper equipment to hang the blinds, thus causing us to have to schedule another appointment.

The second time he came to do the installation, the blinds were not the correct size. He did not even apologize for the incident. His only comment was, "This always happens."

Since this was beginning to unnerve me a bit, I phoned the store and asked to speak to the manager. The man who answered the telephone said that he was too busy and that I would have to speak to an assistant. After explaining my frustration to her and trying to determine a date when the corrected blinds would arrive, it became quite apparent that she did not understand the concept of providing proper customer service.

The next step was to contact the district manager whose answer to the problem was a 10 percent coupon on my next purchase. Are you beginning to see a pattern here?

Usually at this point I will just stop doing business with this type of organization. However, my wife persuaded me to take the problem to a higher level, so I did.

Going one step beyond the district manager, this company offered a "fax the president" phone number to voice any concerns a customer may have. After putting together a letter documenting the unfortunate events, I sent it off to the president just as I had been instructed to do. Surely this would get results. Wrong! It has been more than a year and my wife and I still have not heard back from the president.

It is fairly obvious that we will never again do business with that company again. Since their service standards and the lack of management fostering a service environment seem not to be a concern to them, they are probably not bothered by losing two customers. What should concern them are the hundreds of potential customers who decided not to shop there because of the poor service. How did

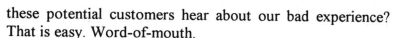

these potential customers hear about our bad experience? That is easy. Word-of-mouth.

Most dissatisfied customers tell nine other people, and a persistent 13 percent of dissatisfied customers tell twenty other people. I fall in the 13 percent category except you can multiply it by many more than twenty.

Had this company acted responsibly at any of the levels where I sought redress, my negative word-of-mouth campaign would probably not be as vocal as it is today.

Ironically, on many occasions this represents an opportunity for the business to win you back. Research has shown that positive word-of-mouth is possible through post complaint response. For many stores, this represents a final chance to win back a customer

Millions of people share their daily experiences at dinner tables, pubs, and offices around the country. What seems as meaningless chatter can result in devastation for an organization that does not foster positive word-of-mouth. In fact studies show that more than 40 percent of Americans seek the advice of friends when shopping for doctors, lawyers, or auto mechanics.

Recently some of my coworkers and I went out to lunch. In the car, the four of us tried to agree on where to go. One person did not like the cleanliness of one of the suggestions while another did not like the slow service. Pow! Just like that, these establishments lost fifty dollars in potential business because of negative word-of-mouth. By now I hope you are starting to understand why each and every Frontcounter™ is crucial to the future success of your business.

When a customer walks into a store, there is a good chance that he or she brings expectations of what level of service they expect to receive. I had the rule at our store that no matter how bad a day a front-liner was having, the worst service he or she could provide was good service. The other 99 percent of the time it should be great service. This great service is what promotes the positive word-of-mouth that brings in new customers.

The customer recognizes great service and that breeds the best type of advertising possible. A print or media advertisement has half the credibility of what your cousin Shirley or uncle Joe has to say. They are powerful walking billboards if treated in a manner that exceeds any expectations they previously had. They also represent potential disaster for those businesses that disappoint their customers.

The most opinionated word-of-mouth comes from those customers scorned by a business. Those customers were treated so poorly or unfairly that they carry an anger that goes far past the exit doors. They will tell as many people as will listen to them why they will not return to your store. Or worse yet, why you should not either. Of the many stores that I have seen go out of business, most all provided this level of service.

Once your organization begins promoting positive word-of-mouth, a new customer base will be developed that will soon shop your place of business. This will result in a perpetual stream of new customers that will expect the great service they heard about. Never, never, never, can you let your guard down since the customers have set their expectations high on the positive word-of-mouth they heard. Because this newly formed base of customers is now shopping your establishment, it becomes more important than ever to continue providing great service.

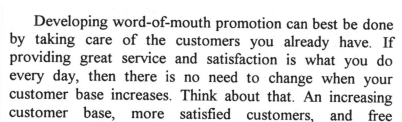

Developing word-of-mouth promotion can best be done by taking care of the customers you already have. If providing great service and satisfaction is what you do every day, then there is no need to change when your customer base increases. Think about that. An increasing customer base, more satisfied customers, and free advertising throughout your neighborhood.

Individuals differ in how they give advice to others. If your business is able to identify these advice givers, then the potential exists to control them. The key to promoting a positive word-of-mouth campaign is to locate these opinion leaders and get them talking about your great service.

Auto Barn, a very successful dealership, is in the business of selling top quality used cars. Positive word-of-mouth had such a valuable impact on bringing in new customers, they were able to cut their advertising expense by 50 percent. I did not buy my car from them but they still offered me the best price available on an extended new car warranty. I know the first place I will shop for my next automobile.

In an age when businesses are constantly scaling back and streamlining their operations, word-of-mouth offers an excellent opportunity to increase your exposure with little or no cost. Managing this program requires performing the fundamentals each day that will differentiate you from others with the great service you will be providing.

Word-of-mouth management should become a daily tool in helping deliver greater customer satisfaction. Although this type of management may seem uncomfortable in the beginning, it will pave the way for huge rewards as your business will continue to grow an increasing customer base.

So, the next time you are at work or walking outside, stop and glance around you. Do you see the same walking billboards I do?

- **Develop a word-of-mouth program for your business by educating the front-liners.**
- **You can promote positive word-of-mouth by exceeding the expectations of your customers.**
- **Word-of-mouth as a marketing tool can greatly reduce the cost of doing business, which is an added benefit to the customer.**

Seven

Memory: The Calculator That Does Not Work

"There is only one boss: the customer. And he can fire everybody in the company, from the chairman on down, simply by spending his money somewhere else."

—Sam Walton

One of the best dining experiences my wife and I have had was at the Chez Paul in downtown Chicago. It's rather on the lavish side but well worth the expense. Of the numerous fine restaurants I have had the opportunity to dine in, this one is very easily the winner in delivering the ultimate in great food and service bar none.

The attention to detail is unmatched. The old mansion where the Chez Paul is located only adds to its charm. Why am I rambling on about a restaurant? Although I would highly recommend this establishment to everyone, if you asked me what I ordered for dinner, I would not remember.

We consumers have very short memories about the facts. It is the service and Frontcounters™ that we remember. How in the world could I spend a hundred dollars on a meal and not remember what I had?

Because the meal was secondary! It is my beautiful wife sitting across from me, the piano man playing soft music, the paintings on the wall, and the waiters never missing a beat that I remember. We went there for dinner, but soon learned it was much more than the food that intrigued us.

This is true of most consumers. They can seldom remember what they bought last at your store, but ask them how they thought the service was. Chances are they remember that very well.

Today's businesses spend countless hours on pricing, displays, inventory, and other important tasks. These are the behind the scenes activities that add to the customers' pleasurable experience. But what they remember most is the condition of the store and how they were treated. Do not believe me? Try this little test.

The last time you went to the store, can you remember everything you bought or do you remember who rung you out? Were the items on sale or did anybody offer you help finding what you needed? If I had a nickel in my pocket, I would bet you cannot remember everything you purchased, but did recall the level of service you received. Especially if it was great service!

There are several deep discount hardware stores in the area surrounding my house. As stated in an earlier chapter, I shop at Home Depot for one reason. They provide the best service. I could not tell you what I paid for some closet shelving that was recently purchased there. But, I do remember the front-liner who helped me locate the aisle it

was found in. I do remember the front-liner who showed me how to install it properly. I do remember the cashier who gave me a certificate to save twenty percent on my next purchase. I also remember the clerk who helped me carry the shelving out to the car and offered to help tie it to the roof.

Studies have shown that customers will remember poor experiences in greater detail than positive ones. Providing great service will give your business an edge in this department. Those that offer average or poor service will have a difficult time winning this battle.

When the customer leaves the store, he or she begins to formulate the total shopping experience in his or her mind. They remember how they were treated from the moment they entered the store to the time they left. It is a little math game we play whether we know it or not. Unfortunately, it does not add up.

Our memories play a little trick on us. That wonderful Frontcounter™ we experienced or that terrific service at the sporting good's store will soon be forgotten if a negative incident occurs before we have left.

Subconsciously we add all the positive experiences that occurred and subtract out the negative ones. For every ten positive ones (an item on sale, a friendly hello, plenty of inventory) it only takes a negative one to wipe them all out.

As you can see, the customer will best remember what the overall score is. Positive or negative. Yes, it takes a greater effort to get a positive reaction from the consumer but the rewards can be unlimited. Do not let all the positive Frontcounters™ and great service you provided throughout their trip be eliminated by one bad experience.

Innovative Medical Services in El Cajun, California wants your experience with their products to be a positive one even after the purchase. They market a pharmaceutical water purification and dispensing system called Fillmaster™. There policy simply states:

If you have questions or encounter any difficulties with your system, please call us first. We made it, and we stand behind it. **PLEASE DON'T CALL A PLUMBER!** Plumbers do not generally understand the workings of our system, and our experience is that they usually give inaccurate diagnoses. Sometimes, they call us when they need help. When they do, we tell them the same thing we would have told you in the first place, and you get a plumbing bill for your trouble. Save yourself a headache and a lot of money. Even if you don't know one end of a screwdriver from the other, call us and we'll either help you fix it yourself or send a replacement part, by Next Day Air if necessary. All we ask you to do is to return the affected part to us. Only in cases of clear abuse or misuse do we charge for this service. Hence our service motto: 'Ship first and ask questions later'. Our telephone number is on the filtration system and it's on the dispenser. You can't lose it. Discover what real customer service is all about, and...PLEASE CALL US FIRST!

Innovative Medical Services understands that the customers needs must be satisfied well after the purchase.

They do not want the customers' last memories of the product to be an unpleasant one.

It should be apparent that providing average service is not going to trigger the customers' memory of their shopping trip. If delighted and treated like this book suggests they should be, you will have a customer who will place your business above the rest in your industry.

Just as the title of this chapter suggests, what a customer remembers about a shopping trip may not add up. The only time the calculator works is when you do not give the customer a chance to have a poor experience.

- **Customers have great memories for what went wrong.**
- **They form a mental report card after they leave your store.**
- **Customers remember great service; not average.**

Eight
_____

What's a Hamburger Without a Bun

"There are many paths to the top of the mountain, but the view is always the same."

—Chinese Proverb

As we discuss great service and the way to achieve it, let us not lose sight of the other factors that make a business successful. It takes careful planning, inventory control, and many other important ingredients. We should maintain the perspective that great service will help our cause enormously but cannot stand on its own. Let me illustrate.

I was leaving on vacation for a few days and brought the car in for a preventative checkup. When I went to pick up the car the next morning, it was not ready. In fact, they had misplaced part of the carburetor and were out of the spark plugs that were needed. After explaining my dilemma to the service manager, he did all he could to locate the missing pieces.

His interest in my problem was genuine and he drove to several stores trying to locate the correct parts. His customer service was exceptional and appreciated; however this could not make up for the mechanics' poor performance. I was supposed to be on vacation but instead was waiting at the service station for my car. It did not matter if they all smiled and charmed me at that point, I still did not have my car.

As you can see, even though the service may be outstanding, the rest of the organization's employees must perform at their end. If you are waiting for an airplane to take off, it will mean little if all the flight attendants are providing great service but the mechanics are unable to fix the problem.

Conversely, on rare occasions great customer service can even bail you out of a situation where a part of the business did not deliver. Here is an example of one such occurrence.

At one of my stores, we operated a one-hour photo machine that allowed us to develop customers' pictures instantly. One day a gentleman brought his camera in and for unexplained reasons, we ruined his film. Unfortunately for both of us, he needed these pictures the next day for a meeting. Well, we really made this customer very angry. Our service was great but we ruined his pictures. After loudly telling me how angry he was, he stormed out of the store before I could offer him compensation of some sort.

At that point I thought we lost a customer because of our dismal performance. I asked my camera front-liner if he could make out any of the images at all on the underdeveloped negatives. He was able to determine that the pictures were all of neon signs around the city of Chicago. I asked the him to fix the one-hour machine and I would be back shortly.

Jumping in the car, I raced throughout the city trying to find the exact locations where he shot all the pictures. I found twelve of the fifteen signs. After returning to the store that evening, the machine was running correctly and we processed the film I had taken earlier.

I called the number that was on the film envelope that he had thrown at me only a few hours earlier. He was not in but I left a message that we have some pictures he may be interested in. A few minutes later he walked in the store to apologize for his anger earlier in the evening, not yet knowing we had called his house to tell him that his pictures were developed.

Today, he is one of the best one-hour photo customers Osco Drug has. He claimed to have had a terrible day before coming to the store and the ruined pictures did not help any. That did not make any difference to the front-liners and me. I have tried to instill in them that any time an area of our business does not live up to the expectations of the customer, drastic measures must be taken immediately.

In this case great service got us out of a jam, but do not count on that happening too often. Many times the customer will not give you a second chance.

While traveling with a group of associates, including the regional vice-president of the southwest region, we decided to stop and get some lunch. We went in to a national chain that is located throughout the United States and boasts of the biggest and best tasting hamburger you will ever eat.

After placing the order, we went to the table and waited for the food. The restaurant was nearly empty and after twenty-five minutes, our food had still not arrived. The regional vice president got up and walked over to the counter to find out what had been taking so long.

The person behind the counter's response to his request was, "Maybe next time you will not order so much." After he told us of this amusing comment, we could only wonder what level customer service plays in the land of the biggest burger.

Front-liners, management, supervisors and all levels that play a role in the organization, are links in the chain that drive the business. When one of these links fails to perform or is not involved in the service commitment of the organization, then a complete customer service program is impossible. All parts must work together and deliver at every possible link.

Remember when the chain used to fall off your bike and it was inoperable until you got off and put it back on. The same is true of your business. This is why the front-liners play such a crucial role in the daily operations in a service environment. Understand that the team is a unit and its members independently will struggle when all are not working together for the same purpose.

On numerous occasions, I can recall a terrific customer service experience ruined by an area of the business that failed to deliver.

During a vacation in Australia, we stayed at a hotel that claimed to be one of the best around. From its magnificent lobby entrance to its perfectly polished elevators, this hotel had all the makings for a perfect stay. However, these wonderful amenities could not make up for the poor housekeeping, loud construction noises and terrible front-desk service.

Strive to offer the customer a complete package of products and services to choose from and then deliver it. Exceed their expectations at all levels of the business and you will find not only repeat customers but new ones amazed at what they see. When there is an opportunity for improvement in a particular area, address it immediately. Don't just plug the hole. Repair it!

This chapter begins by asking the question, "What is a hamburger without a bun?" Understanding that great service alone (the hamburger), without the support of the entire team (the bun), will leave the customer hungry. If you are like me, do not stop there. Go ahead and put on all the extras!

- **All levels of the organization must perform to deliver great customer service.**
- **Failing to deliver in a particular area, like a disease, will spread if not fixed.**
- **Great service cannot stand on its own.**

Nine
Front-line Math

"You can dream, create, design, and build the most wonderful place in the world, but it requires people to make the dream a reality."

−Walt Disney

L et's say your front-line employees have fifty Frontcounters™ at the checkstand each day. Now let's say that the average customer spends a $1,000 a year in your store. That front-liner you were viewing as a five dollar an hour employee has now become a $1 million account representative. (fifty customers a day x $1,000 x 240 days.)

Now if you are still struggling with the front-liner being a major contributor to your organization, please reread the first paragraph until it becomes clearer.

Ten

Empowerment: Everyone Wears a Sheriff's Badge

"You have to have the confidence not just in your own abilities but in those of the people around you."

–Joe Montana

When I was a junior in high school, my summer job consisted of working at a concession stand on the beach in Chicago. As a young very hormonal teenager, there was no better job one could have.

One very busy, very hot Saturday afternoon, my manager at the time decided after a long conversation with a blonde in a bathing suit, that the hot-dog and soda business was no longer very important. He tossed the keys and told me to run the place while he went off gallivanting with his new friend. It was at that point that I discovered the meaning of empowerment.

Yes, I agree that selling a few hot-dogs and sodas while the boss is away was not the most pressure sensitive moment I have ever experienced. However it did make me aware very quickly that any decision that would be made, crucial or not, would have to come from me.

I have spoken to many front-liners who themselves have been empowered in this sort of fashion. Whether it is somebody tossing you a set of keys or a manager recklessly abandoning you when the angriest customer in town approaches, this type of empowerment program is not conducive to great customer service.

Empowerment is the direct result of proper training. When the front-liner receives proper instruction and is given the authority to correct a customer concern on the spot, both the customer and business are winners.

Many managers have a hard time when they empower or trust front-liners with some decision making processes. These are typically the managers who do not spend time properly working with the front-liners. With some training comes the confidence to make good decisions. When we empower front-liners, we are telling them that there is a level of trust that they have earned. When we empower them and they have not received the proper training, the customer will be the first one to notice.

If you have ever been on a trail horse, you know that they are smarter than their riders on many occasions. If you do not let the horse know that you are confident in your riding abilities and show control, you may be in for a long afternoon. The horse has the ability to know when the rider is a novice. It can be a light hold on the reins or the legs not tucked securely against the horse's side. These are the signs to the horse that you are not in control.

Although this may sound strange, the customers are very similar to horses. They know when the person empowered to solve their problems is not in control. On numerous occasions I have gone to get a refund and the person who came up to wait on me was not empowered to handle the situation. I have had front-liners tell me that without a register receipt they are not allowed to give exchanges under any circumstances.

It is difficult for the customer to take your business very seriously when the front-liners cannot instantly correct a problem. As a store manager, it was my philosophy that the employees could make decisions at the store that they felt were in the best interest of the customer. They did not have to come to Brian for permission or any other managers on duty. They were empowered to correct all problems right on the spot.

If they were unsure of a procedure or felt that management might chose an alternative remedy, the front-liners were then instructed to call a manager. Ninety-five percent of the time they were able to solve the problem without getting on the intercom and letting the entire store know that a refund was needed or could a manager come to the service desk. If I am shopping in a store and that call comes over the intercom, I want to run up there and see if it is a situation that maybe the front-liner could have handled.

When studying the components that make up a high-performance customer driven team, it became apparent to me that they all shared a common characteristic. Each of the successful teams were set up to have the fewest layers possible. This in turn reduced the time and resources associated with approvals and other decisions. These teams were better able to work together as they emphasized interaction and teamwork.

Apply a strategy to make sure that the front-liners responsible for customer contacts have the necessary tools and decision-making power to properly service the customer during this contact. Once you are able to identify the needs of the customer, then set up a service quality delivery system to ensure that the team is meeting the customers' needs.

Do not let this empowerment program stop with the store team. Customer empowerment is also an effective tool in providing better service. Businesses that are committed to gaining an advantage will show their customers how to serve themselves. With this option, you gain a competitive advantage both in terms of increased customer satisfaction and more streamlined operations.

Many a wise manager has found that properly giving power to others in the organization will allow them greater time in serving the needs of the customers. As these businesses begin to flatten their organizational structure, they have found middle managers and front-liners becoming even more important in the day-to-day decision-making process.

A gentleman who I was having dinner with in Boston told an amusing tale of why he would no longer stay at the hotel he had lodged at on his previous trip.

It seems he flew in late the night before and was unable to get dinner before checking into the hotel. He decided to grab breakfast at the hotel early in the morning before he traveled into the city for an early morning meeting. After arriving at the location where a free continental breakfast was to be served, he soon discovered it did not open for another ten minutes.

He explained to the young woman at the counter that he was in a hurry to get to a meeting in the city and would like to grab a muffin and a cup of coffee before catching a cab. She explained to him that she was not allowed to let anyone in before it was time. Although he was within arm's length of the muffin, it made no difference. My friend checked out of the hotel that evening and has never been there since.

Was this a front-liner who did not understand the potential business this muffin episode might jeopardize or was she not empowered to fix the problem? Whatever the case, the hotel lost a very good customer. In fact, make that two.

- **Include all levels in the decision-making responsibilities.**
- **Set up a service quality delivery system that allows the team to fix the problems.**
- **Empowerment involves proper training and instruction.**

Eleven

Rules: Service sTRONG Enough to Bend

"Good judgment is to business what good steering is to navigation."

–Henry Ward Beecher

I felt a little nervous about writing this chapter at first. You might agree it's not common practice to tell your employees that breaking rules is O.K. That is not what I want to talk about. Rather this is about encouraging the front-liners to take chances doing extraordinary feats that produce amazing results.

Having the opportunity to open up many new stores all over the country, I have been afforded a unique view of the front-line service even before the store is opened. Let me set the stage.

It was late February 1993, the day before we were to open a new store on the South Side of Chicago. It was very icy out and since the store was not opening until the following day the outdoor lights were not on. I will let Mr. Accetturo tell the rest of the story.

On and off, throughout my seventy-one years of living on this earth I have come across individuals who took the time, the one step or several steps to go beyond or out of their way to help others.

Not earthshaking or glory-seeking, just simple acts of kindness.

On February 24, I drove into the parking lot of Osco Drug to pick up a transistor radio battery for my small radio. After carefully walking across the ice, I reached the door and to my surprise the door was locked. The store was not due to open until February 25th, and I did not see the sign.

A young man came to the door, opened it, and inquired as to my needs. I told him what I needed. Although the store was closed, he let me in, sold me my small battery, let me walk across the front of the store to avoid walking on the ice which was a shorter distance to the car. He told me to come back the next day as the ice would be removed and free gifts were to be handed out.

No! Brian could have turned me away and I could have walked away and made my purchase elsewhere.

Brian Dennis took one step beyond, saw my struggle, came to my aid and did a simple act of kindness toward his fellow man.

Oh, yes, I did go back to Osco the following day and the ice was removed from the lot. I did take a tour of the store and by the time I had left, I had dropped a hefty amount of coins into the till, to the tune of $70.85. I shall highly recommend to my friends, neighbors, and coworkers the virtues of the behavior of the employees of Osco Drug.

I shall pass this world but once. Any good, therefore that I can do, or any kindness that I can show to any human being, let me do it now. Let me not defer or neglect it, for I may not pass this way again.

This letter is posted on my office wall for many reasons. First, it reminds me every day that front-liners who are able to react to unique situations have the opportunity to win a customer for life. It tells the customer that their unusual request or situation will be dealt with in a professional manner. No organization is too large to cater to the special needs of its customers.

Secondly, it reinforces the concept of leading by example. The supervisor of the store was less than ten feet away when I opened up the door and let Mr. Accetturo get his battery. You could see in her eyes that she did not understand why I let this customer into the store when it had not even been opened yet. She turned to me after he left and asked, "Why would you let a customer in when the store has not even opened for business yet?" I told her, "It is simple. If you owned this business and this gentleman came to your store, what would you do?"

I am not sure she truly understood my actions until she saw the letter that Mr. Accetturo sent the vice-president of Chicagoland operations for Osco Drug. It was then that she began to understand the importance of giving that extra effort.

Let's look at another example.

When I asked my wife to marry me, I did so at the one place in the world that was both beautiful and meaningful to both of us. You see, Pam and I both love great wine and one of our favorites is Robert Mondavi. My wine representative at the time arranged a phone call between the winery and me. The first example of great service was the wine representative going outside his everyday responsibilities to make his customer (me) happy.

After careful planning between Michelle Davis, the tour guide at the winery, and myself, it was now time to surprise my wife with tickets to San Francisco for the weekend. After spending a day in the city, we moved on to Napa Valley, California where the big surprise awaited. At this point, Pam just thought we were going for a nice tour of the winery.

Michelle greeted us at the entrance and I slipped her the engagement ring while Pam used the ladies room to freshen up before the tour began. Soon after, the three of us began our private tour of one of the world's most gorgeous wineries.

A few hours later we were escorted to the private dining room that overlooked the entire winery. We were treated like royalty, sipping several different wines and feasting on one of the finest lunches I have ever had. The plan was going along perfectly.

After lunch, Michelle suggested we take a walk and see the different grapes surrounding the vineyard. Pam, still not

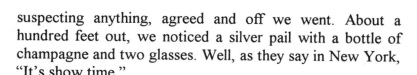

suspecting anything, agreed and off we went. About a hundred feet out, we noticed a silver pail with a bottle of champagne and two glasses. Well, as they say in New York, "It's show time."

I did the honorable knee drop and asked my wife to marry me. Her reaction time was a just little slower than I had liked (the several glasses of wine might have had something to do with it) but a few seconds later I got the answer I was looking for and we were soon celebrating the memorable occasion.

As we walked back, the entire winery staff applauded and presented us with an autographed bottle of wine from Robert Mondavi himself. As are most winning accomplishments, it was a total team effort to make this day so special.

I share this personal story with you because it illustrates that an individual went out of her normal scope of responsibilities to accommodate a customer's needs. From the moment Michelle and I spoke on the phone, she had a "Whatever I can do" attitude to make the engagement a success. Pam and I were honored to be the first couple ever to get engaged at the winery. They could have told us, "No, we do not do that sort of thing" or "We do not have the time." Instead they accommodated the customer's needs down to the last detail.

This success story does not end after we left the winery. On our wedding day, Robert Mondavi sent us a case of his private reserve wine with a note extending his congratulations. Unlike many businesses out there today, the winery delivered extraordinary service that exceeded our expectations. When we have a dinner party or are out at a restaurant, which wine do you think accompanies our meal?

When a business creates an environment in which the front-liners feel they are important to the company's success, they will feel less attached to the chains of limitations. The front-liners should not be hindered by a management team that discourages the bending of rules to give quality service. Instead, the employee should be rewarded and encouraged to find intangible ways of achieving superior service. This does not mean throwing the company's procedure book out the window, but rather finding new ways to delight the customer that may be unorthodox at best.

This type of rule-bending service cannot be taught. It needs to breed and foster in the store team. Management cannot tell front-liners that a unique service situation might come up some day and expect them to break the rules if need be. This type of service must be practiced every day by everybody on the team. The managers and supervisors can only illustrate this with each and every Frontcounter™ they have.

In Kansas, a sudden and unpredictable downpour soaked nearly all of Sun Newspapers papers as they lay on porches and lawns in the early morning of Wednesday, June 28, 1995. The publisher, Steve Rose, ordered an immediate recall and reprinted the entire run of 100,000 newspapers.

He did not need to read a rule book or consult lawyers to make his decision. He knew that his readers and advertisers demanded attention and he provided it. Steve was not obligated to reprint the run but he bent the rules to provide the ultimate service to his customers.

When you are at the bottom of a mountain it's relatively easy to take risks. As you climb up to greater heights, it becomes more difficult. In life, I enjoy operating at the top of the mountain. This can be accomplished because of a

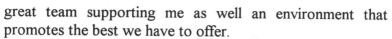

great team supporting me as well an environment that promotes the best we have to offer.

Taking risks is scary enough. Taking them in an environment that adds little support is even more frightening. We are only as good as the front-liners working beside us. So, get those shoes on and start climbing that mountain. One Frontcounter™ at a time.

- **Over the top customer service sometimes requires radical approaches to unique situations.**
- **Bending the rules to please a customer should be encouraged.**
- **A risk-taking environment should be encouraged to promote the ultimate in service potential.**

Twelve

No Signs!
Take Them All Down

"Destiny is not a matter of chance; it is a matter of choice. It is not something to be waited for, but rather something to be achieved."
—Alfred North Whitehead

After visiting some of our stores in Las Vegas, I wanted to get some dinner at a restaurant off the strip, thus avoiding the crowds. Not very familiar with the area, I asked the concierge where he recommended for a quick bite to eat. After heeding his advice, I went to a small Italian restaurant down the street.

Before even walking into this restaurant there were two "**No**" signs on the front door! No credit cards or checks accepted and no patrons under 18 without adult supervision. Normally I would have walked away at that point but I was hungry and it was getting late.

Inside the restaurant, there was another sign that read, "A minimum gratuity of 16 percent will be added to all checks no matter what the party size." After noticing the sign I asked the hostess who was beginning to seat me if that applied to me since I was by myself. She replied, "The sign's pretty clear isn't it?" I was quickly starting to lose my appetite at this point but stayed because it could not get much worse than this.

Well, I was wrong. When the waiter came to take my order, I asked him if I could get a glass of water. He looked up and pointed to the sign on the wall that stated "The only water we serve is bottled." I asked him if this is complimentary and he replied "No, but it's only $1.50." If the straw broke the camel's back, this sign broke mine.

After staring for a minute or so in disbelief, I put my napkin down and told the waiter I was not very hungry anymore. The part that shocked me most was the fact that he did not seem bothered by my sudden departure. He just went to the next table.

I have a theory. It is simply that the amount of "no" signs a business has is directly indicative of the service you can probably expect to receive. Yes, I understand that certain situations may warrant the necessity of such signs. However, the 99 percent of all other businesses out there do not have an excuse.

Why in the world would you ever want to tell a customer "no"? We work too hard to get the customer in the door. These signs only distance the customer from your business. To date, I have not seen a "no" sign that leaves me with a warm feeling. Rather they are almost insulting to what I regard as customer satisfaction.

Let me give you some examples of my theory in action.

After attending a wedding reception in Omaha, Nebraska, my wife and I did some shopping in the old downtown warehouse district. Pam loves antiques so we decided to stop at a few of the stores.

Before entering one of the antique stores, I noticed on the door they had an unusual amount of "no" signs posted. Upon entering the store there were "no" signs all over. They were hanging from the ceiling, attached to the walls and taped to the tables. Nothing was excluded. Some included "No touching; If you break it you bought it; Shoplifters will be shot; No children under 16 without parents; Absolutely, positively if you drop it – you own it." This book is not long enough to include all the signs Pam and I read that day.

As we neared the checkout, we could see the owner behind the counter looking out over the merchandise wondering why nobody seemed to be buying anything. As we left the store, I could only hope that she studied the customers who were studying all those no signs.

Here is one more.

After going into one of our competitors' stores, I noticed a handwritten sign at the checkout that stated, "Absolutely no refunds without a receipt. No exceptions!" I wish all our competition would have this sign posted. This was too good to pass up. I had to test this rule of theirs.

I purchased some film and the next day went to return it. There's only one catch. I was going to try and get my money back without a receipt. Surely a businessperson in a suit should be able to get $4.25 back without much resistance.

I walked to the service counter where I asked the clerk if this is where I can return something. Without even looking up she asked if I had a receipt. I responded no. She then rattled off the policy that I had read the previous day. Not happy with her response, I asked her if I could speak with the manager. Angrily she called the manager to the service desk.

When he asked if he could help me, I repeated my story of wanting to return this unused film. He recited (although not as well as the clerk) their policy on refunds. If you only knew how much I was actually enjoying this. He said the best he could offer me was an in-store credit for the film purchase. Turning to him very calmly, I asked, "Are you willing to lose a customer over this ridiculous policy?" His response was "I guess I am."

At that point I produced my receipt and kindly asked for my money back. I wish each one of you could have seen the look on his face and the others who worked there. He stormed away and told the clerk to give me my money back.

About six months later I went back to the store to see if that sign was still posted at the checkstand. Yes, it was still there, except now they had a frame around it. They must have been very proud of that sign.

Welcome the customer. Statistics show customers decide in the first eight seconds of a shopping trip if they feel comfortable or not. Put up "yes" signs.

Yes, we offer complete satisfaction.

Yes, our goal is to make you happy.

Yes, we have extended hours.

Now is that not much better than being greeted by no this and no that? I look forward to doing business with those organizations that make me feel welcome.

Take a good look around your business and see how many "no" signs are hanging about. If the customer is going to perceive this sign in a way not consistent with the level of

service you hope to deliver, I strongly recommend taking them down. Remember the goal is to welcome customers; not show them the rule book.

- "No" signs give the customer a negative impression.
- They form a barrier between you and the customer.
- The customer may develop mixed service messages.
- "No" signs are directly proportionate to the expected level of service.

Thirteen

Catering to the Mature Customer

"Outwardly I am 83, but inwardly I am every age, with the emotions and experiences of each period."

—Elizabeth Coatsworth

"You know you're getting old when you stoop down to tie your shoes and wonder what else you can do when you're down there."

—George Burns

The 62 million – one of every four people in the United States – who are age 50 and over represent a huge and profitable market for today's products and services. It is difficult to lump and generalize 62 million mature adults whose only common denominator is that they were born prior to 1946. However, recent developments in the mature market suggest that the companies out there are beginning to take notice.

Most of the major department stores and shopping powerhouses offer discounts and advantages to their mature customers. These programs showcase the importance of this group as the retailers struggle to target this fast growing age group. Businesses have only begun to understand what it takes to satisfy this group and the privileges that come from being a mature customer.

Our thought process has become imprisoned by the word senior as it is used to describe the older adults in our society. I do not like the word senior for many reasons. The term has acquired a narrow meaning that reflects negatively on the individuality, intelligence, and human potential of those to whom it is applied.

My grandmother, who is 77 years old, has a positive outlook toward the future as most mature adults do. Our family pokes good natured fun at my younger brother who will often come home on a Friday night and take a nap. This is so he is not tired when he has to pick up our grandmother at her Friday night dance at midnight! Does this sound like a senior to you?

In this book, the phrase mature adults will represent the over 50 population. Putting them into a category is like combining the characteristics of the 20-50 consumer. For our purposes in discussing how to properly serve this group, the term mature adult will suffice. Mature adulthood is not necessarily an age; rather it is a stage of life. Each of us enters this stage at different times of our lives.

Later in chapter 24, you will be introduced to Millie Lutzow. Millie is a front-liner 84 years young who delighted us with her service skills while stopping for a quick bite to eat. As she says "I love people and making them happy during the few moments we meet makes my day."

In today's marketplace, if you are not focusing on the mature adult, you could possibly be missing one of the most profitable target groups out there. Although typically more demanding than younger shoppers, these adults account for a growing number of dollars being spent every year.

Many characteristics form the makeup of these shoppers. They generally require more time from clerks and salespeople. They also tend to shop with a greater frequency than younger shoppers. These mature adults not only shop more often but frequently do their shopping trips earlier in the day when the stores are less busy. As one of my customers once told me, "Seniors are not difficult to satisfy; they simply know what they want."

Charlie Peterson was a retired international accountant who did all his morning shopping needs at my store in downtown Chicago. The store opened every morning at seven o'clock and Charlie was there waiting. If the store was not in ready to shop condition, he let you know it.

Occasionally, I would ask Charlie to critique the store with me and discuss opportunities that would make his shopping experience more enjoyable. When we did this, he always insisted on starting outside of the store about fifty feet from the entrance. Charlie explained that his first impression of the store that morning would be made at this distance.

One early morning in midsummer, Charlie and I were evaluating the store's appearance from the outside when he said, "Brian, do you know the letter h on your pharmacy drive-through sign has been burned out for two days now?" Since I arrived at work a few hours before the store opened and the lights were not activated that early, I had failed to recognize the sign problem. It immediately became apparent to me that Charlie's perception of the store was formed well before he entered the door.

> **THE SHOPPER HAS ALREADY FORMED AN ASSESSMENT OF YOUR BUSINESS EVEN BEFORE THE FIRST FRONTCOUNTER™.**

Businesses today spend thousands of dollars every year on consulting fees. My consultant was Charlie Peterson and I did not have to pay him a cent. If you ask your mature customers to take a few minutes evaluating the store showing you what they like or dislike, you may never need another consultant again.

I would offer some of the more frequent shoppers ten dollars in cash if they would share with me what they disliked about my store. As of today, I have not met a consultant who could advise me as well as they did for that price. Although mature shoppers can be more demanding, they can also offer you a greater insight into your business.

Today when you turn on any television or radio, you are bombarded by companies trying to win your business with sales, price reductions or so called close-outs. These sales tactics are important tools for reaching the mature customer, but it takes more than price to keep them coming back.

Many of my older shoppers were viewed by the front-liners as comparative price and sale conscious. Price represents only part of the winning formula. The amenities and personal Frontcounters™ that they carry with them as

they leave the store all contribute to a pleasurable shopping experience.

The U.S. Census Bureau estimates that by the year 2050, 24.3 percent of the population will be 65 or older. That is compared with 1995's estimated 13.2 percent. This projected increase is staggering. This group is growing faster than the general population. Is your business preparing to identify and serve this group of shoppers?

The mature customer is afforded a new way to shop that is dramatically different from previous means. The number of things that we can buy today in contrast to what our customers could buy only a few years ago is mindboggling. The mature customer living in a metropolitan area with a population of more than a million has access to more than a million consumer products and thousands of merchants.

At Wal-Mart's HyperMart alone, a customer can select from nearly 110,000 different products in 130,000 square feet. Only a few years ago, this type of selection did not exist. Not only is your business adjusting to a new shopper, but they in turn are adjusting to the new businesses.

Do not be fooled by the mature shoppers. They are often more educated and intune with the pricing and service your organization provides than most. Underestimating this group may prove fatal. They understand an "every-day price versus the constant sale price." Studies have shown that once this group of shoppers feels cheated, it will take many dollars to win them back.

Over the course of my career, I have met many mature adults who amazed me with their positive outlook toward the future. This group is active, caring, and a force to be reckoned with. They provided my store team with valuable lessons that can only come from experience.

In any event, the willingness of an organization to succeed is directly proportionate to their willingness to listen. Our mature customers have fond memories of the days of personal service and someone who would listen. This group requires the best service our front-liners can possibly give. Catering to this group means learning to satisfy its needs. This can only be accomplished by listening and reacting.

- Catering to your mature customers will yield huge dividends.
- Understand their needs and then deliver the extraordinary service to meet them.
- Tap into the enormous potential input your mature shoppers can offer.

Fourteen

Front-line Ideas:
A Lesson in Listening

"The secret of success in life is for man to be ready for his opportunity when it comes."

                                                      –Benjamin Disraeli

One of the greatest compliments I have received in my career came from a 19-year-old stock clerk who worked in one of our Chicago area stores. I had just finished a discussion with the pharmacist on duty when this stock clerk commented to me "You remind me of a four year old who is beginning to explore the world for the first time."

I did not quite understand why she was comparing me to a four year old so I asked her to explain. She said "You are always asking us questions and what we think about this and that. Sometimes I think we are the ones who manage the store." You know something? She was absolutely right and I loved it.

Winning At The Front-line

The front-liners who worked with me had a lot to say about how the store was run. Their ideas and comments were valuable tools that I was constantly tapping into. Call me a four year old or a pest with a lot of questions, but I can tell you one thing. I always listened!

In a survey of workers, the United States Chamber of Commerce and the Gallup Organization found that 72 percent spend at least some time thinking about ways to improve their organization. That is a large group of front-liners who could provide valuable ideas and suggestions that will instantly improve the way you are doing business today. If that statistic did not shake you a little bit, let me offer you another. Almost three-fourths of your store team has ideas to offer your business if you are willing to listen.

In our society today, we have the perception that the managers are all knowing. Of the employees surveyed above, only 29 percent saw any chance of the organization acting on their ideas. Do the front-liners not have any good suggestions? Have they not received the proper schooling to offer intelligent ideas? Or do we have imbedded in us a traditional approach between management and employee?

Today, the successful companies are the ones that are customer and employee driven. These companies are open to employee ideas and concerns. The businesses that want to survive well into the next century better understand the limitations that accompany the traditional management focused organization.

Many of these organizations are set up so the front-liners are expected to act in a predetermined way that will penalize them for any actions not viewed as consistent with the traditional thinking. This type of thought process is to blame for much of the poor service you may have experienced with the government sector of the work force.

94

Listening to the front-liners requires more than just listening. It needs to be a two way communication of ideas, concerns, and comments. In fact you may find many of their suggestions run parallel to those of your customers.

For years, the General Motors division of Cadillac has been fighting an aging customer base that is slipping away. They are now trying to attract young buyers including women and minorities, in part with sleeker, smaller cars.

Cadillac will introduce its first new model in more than a decade, called Catera. Cadillac spent months and many resources on an outside image consultant testing possible names but opted for Catera. Now who do you think came up with the name? No, not the expensive consultants General Motors had originally hired. Rather it was a GM employee.

For now, we need to get a basic understanding why we have struggled in the past tapping into the expertise our front-liners encompass. If us so-called managers could learn to check our egos at the door when we walk into our businesses each morning, then maybe we can begin to discover the potential that exists in our own backyard. Do not get me wrong. It will not be easy to correct thinking that has lasted well over a century.

Once the barriers begin to fall, then the front-liners will be more willing to come forward with some great ideas. Listening to their concerns and ideas is as important to a service environment as listening to patients is to good health care.

I had a front-liner who made a suggestion at one of my stores that netted us an extra $18,000 a year pure profit to the bottom line. He approached me after the store had closed and we were cleaning up for the evening. His idea was the result of the comments some of his friends made a few days earlier.

Since the store was located in a very busy night life area of downtown Chicago where there was very little parking, he suggested that we rent out the lot to a valet service after the store closed at night. A few phone calls and a couple of signatures later, we were in the valet business. Our customers appreciated it, too.

As the retail environment becomes more competitive, it becomes crucial to keep current with the latest trends. I have found this especially true in clothing and child oriented items. Many times if we listen to our front-liners, they will tell us what is "hot" and "in" that might otherwise take months to learn if we went the traditional route.

My front-liners were excited to be the first in the area to offer a new item before anyone else had it. It was their version of the stock market and they enjoyed it. By no means am I telling you each and every item was a winner. But the vast majority provided substantial earnings before the market became diluted.

The customers also recognized that our store had new and exciting merchandise before most other retailers. You can bet I relied on the front-liners to keep our store current with the right product mix for a rapidly changing retail market.

When the front-liners see that their ideas are being applied, they gain an enthusiasm that is difficult to match. There is a sense of pride the front-liners get when they see their ideas on the store shelves or a suggestion that management soon implemented.

This ocean of employee ideas will dry up if they feel as a whole they are ignored. Encouraging feedback also carries with it the responsibility of following through on their concerns. "If this were your store, what would you do differently" approach may be the best way to encourage ideas if you find the front-liners are not readily offering any. Just like any team, they need to feel their suggestions are taken seriously and implemented if they offer the best solution.

A front-liner who exhibits greater enthusiasm is more likely to provide a superior customer service environment. When the front-liner comes up with a good idea, make sure he or she is congratulated and encouraged to offer more. You will soon see it easily becomes contagious when the rest of the team witnesses these events.

Whether sixteen or seventy year old front-liners work along with us, it remains important to solicit feedback and encourage ideas that will enable us to run better stores. These ideas will not only allow you to run a better business, but may provide new and exciting services to your customers.

Now it's up to you to find the ideas. The best place to start is with the front-liners. Trust me! The ideas are out there, so go listen up.

- **Seek front-line ideas.**
- **Operate in an environment that encourages employee ideas to offer greater customer satisfaction.**
- **Establish a reward/ bonus system for winning suggestions.**

Fifteen

The Art of Having Fun At Work

If it isn't fun, why do it?

—Operating slogan of Ben & Jerry's

So now you have made it to the chapter that talks about having fun at work. Has the author lost his marbles?

You are probably saying to yourself that having fun and the service industry should never be used in the same sentence, let alone in the same book. Right? Not necessarily.

There is a secret to having fun at work. I will share it with you now, but you must be careful because it can be awfully contagious. Are you ready? It's one simple word. Attitude!

It means going to work every day surrounded by management and front-liners who also share your attitude.

It's being given the opportunity to be yourself and look at "work life" from a different perspective. It is the environment that we all would like to be in if we could not be out doing our favorite activity.

Most of us have to work for a living. I keep trying but I have not won the lottery yet. The next best thing is to create a work situation that enables me to enjoy myself until the winning ticket comes through.

A good friend of mine has a theory. You work one-third of your life, you play one-third of your life, and you sleep one-third of your life. Mine is a little bit different. I play two-thirds of my life and there is only one way to do that. By having fun at work.

For those of you who hate your jobs, there is probably little here that I could say to change your opinion.

However, if you are one of the millions of front-liners who would enjoy your job if it was structured a little differently, then these next few pages are for you. When a front-liner comes to work, it should be a natural extension of his or her personality when not at work. That is, we should encourage the entire team to build an environment that will allow for expression and creativity.

When I was a store manager, this was the attitude I tried to share with my front-liners. In the retail industry, it is a pretty simple concept. Have what the customer wants, when they want it, and provide the best service possible while giving it to them.

Stocking shelves can be the most mundane task out there. How can I make a repetitive task like stocking fun? By changing the attitude surrounding the job at hand. That is, by positioning the job role to accommodate the needs of the front-liner, which better aligns the effort and commitment needed to get the job done.

My front-liners would often tell me that they enjoyed coming to work because they felt they were being paid to have fun. Remember when you were ten and your parents took you to the carnival? You may have been there for three hours but it seemed like five minutes because you had so much fun. My front-liners wanted this type of store to work in and I gave it to them.

Now I know some of you are still a little skeptical at this point. That is all right. You may not be used to having a good time at work and it might take a little longer to convert you. All I ask is that you give the store team a chance to enjoy themselves while getting the job done. The results will astound you. Let's look at an example.

Tuesday was warehouse night in the store, and there would be twenty pallets of product to put out before the end of the evening. This required ten front-liners and me to get an enormous amount of work done in a relatively short amount of time. We would accomplish this week in and week out and still have a great time filling the shelves.

It is the attitude my front-liners had before they walked into the store that day. I was on the sales floor working right beside them on these warehouse nights having just as much fun as they were. If they could have this much fun on a warehouse night with their boss in the next aisle, they could have just as much fun on another night when I was not there and it would be O.K.

We all want to work at a place where we can enjoy our jobs but do not have to feel that each and every move needs to be rehearsed or organized. I found the front-liners greatly increased their productivity when they were allowed to work in an environment that let them be themselves. The customer picks up on this attitude and begins to see the store team "family" that works there.

My wife has this philosophy that everyone who is at the ice cream shop is glad to be there. She says, "You never see an unhappy face."

After laughing for a few seconds, I realized she was right. Can you say the same about your business? Are the front-liners and customers both enjoying themselves throughout the day? Is there a happy and pleasant attitude throughout the store?

Mirage Resorts, which owns and operates the Mirage, Treasure Island, and the Golden Nugget, has 30 million annual visitors to its properties, which offer volcano eruptions, pirate battles and nightclub shows. Even with all these spectacular events, Mirage Resorts knows these attractions will only bring people to its resorts once, possibly twice, if they do not visit regularly.

In a highly competitive environment called the Las Vegas strip, Mirage Resorts has recognized that ultimately, the front-liners make the difference. The frontdesk personnel, change vendors and restaurant hosts are all taught to put their personalities to work and have fun. With this thinking in place, the employees and customers are both winners.

Coming up through the ranks, I had the opportunity to work for several different managers. Each had an individual style and philosophy dealing with the front-liners and the type of store they ran. I learned a lot from all of them. Some good and some not so good.

The managers who created an environment that made front-liners feel comfortable and thus enjoy their jobs more, had greater success in having a store that required little management direction. These front-liners had a more closely knit group than other store teams. They developed a bond with each other that is typically found in environment's front-liners create when they find satisfaction and enjoyment in their jobs.

The employees at the stores that operate with the understanding that having fun while accomplishing the task at hand is acceptable, will outlast the industry average. One of the biggest complaints among management today is the enormous turnover. They claim that finding employees who will stay longer than six months is getting more difficult every day. Giving great service with a constantly changing employee base poses extra challenges.

I did not see this as a problem at the stores that had a front-line team who enjoyed themselves at work. The managers at these stores knew if they let the front-liners operate in a store that directly reflects a happy attitude, this would not be a job they come to every day. Rather it is a place where they are proud to work and maybe somehow, someway, sometime, even try to have a little fun along the way.

- **Create an environment that allows the front-liners to enjoy their work. This will be viewed by customers as a fun place to shop.**
- **A family oriented team will outperform a group of individuals.**
- **Having fun + getting the job done = happy employees.**

Sixteen

Bathrooms: Can We Talk?

"Most of us are about as eager to be changed as we were to be born, and go through our changes in a similar state of shock."
— James Baldwin

Don't laugh. The manner in which your business attends to the neatness of the bathrooms, probably says a lot about your level of concern for the customer. Some people believe in this, while others neglect the entire notion. If you do not have the same concern level I do, maybe two experts in the field can convince you. The customer and my wife Pam.

You see, Pam is a lieutenant commander in the United States Navy Nurse Corps. In her twelve years of military health care service, she has learned the meaning of immaculate bathrooms. Conversely, she has taught many young recruits that anything less than a perfect bathroom is unacceptable. Since she was a pro in this arena, I suggested when we got married that maybe she should be in charge of that part of the house. Unfortunately for me, that logic did not sail with her.

I am not saying that your bathrooms require the same standards of the United States Navy, but they should leave a lasting impression on the customers who use them. How many times have you used a bathroom that was filthy and not well managed? Did it leave you with a few concerns about the establishment as well, especially if it was in the food service industry?

I can name a few local restaurants that my wife and I would never patronize again because of the poor bathroom facilities. One of the restaurants had excellent food, but after the dining experience, my friend came back to the table saying how deplorable the bathrooms were. That fine meal did not quite taste the same anymore.

Hardee's, a fast food chain with more than 4,000 outlets, recently instituted a new management team to rescue this organization from falling sales and earnings. With earnings running 50 percent behind the previous year, this new management team would have to take a roll-up-the-sleeves approach to running the outlets.

The new chief operating officer, Raymond J. Perry, did not wait long to show his team that attention to detail would be a must at all Hardee's locations. Mr. Perry scrubbed toilets in a Hardee's in Florida that did not meet his standards. "The word spread very quickly" he says of the exercise. He knew that once the front-liners and management saw this effort of commitment coming from an executive, they would soon share a similar pledge for excellence. Although Hardee's has many challenges to work

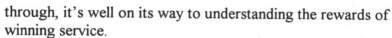

through, it's well on its way to understanding the rewards of winning service.

I worked for a manager who took the bathrooms so seriously that he hired an employee for the sole purpose of keeping them spotless. This employee was the slowest worker I had ever seen. On one occasion I asked my manager if we could terminate him since he took three hours to clean two bathrooms.

The manager brought me downstairs where the bathrooms were located and asked me if I had ever seen a bathroom cleaner than those. I replied, "No." He then explained to me that even though it may take him a little longer than most to clean the bathrooms, nobody does it better. He said, "You see Brian, when the customers see and smell our bathrooms, they are also evaluating the store. Why would you jeopardize what we work so hard for on the sales floor with less than perfect facilities? Sometimes this is the customer's last remembrance of the store and we should make it a positive one."

That manager taught me a great deal about how important the little pieces of the big puzzle are. Until you have that last piece, the puzzle is not finished.

After traveling to some of our locations in California, five of us boarded the van that took us to the stores. After visiting one of the stores, the regional vice president looked back to one of the women in the van who used the bathroom in the store and asked her about its condition. She hesitated and told him it was O.K. He told her the men's was in very poor condition. We all knew when he said that, somebody was going to be receiving a not-so-nice phone call.

Many in the van seemed startled that the regional vice-president was getting upset about a bathroom. Only after a lengthy dinner conversation did they begin to understand its importance from a customer standpoint.

Many restaurants keep a log on the back of the door indicating the last time it was cleaned and by whom. If a log works for your business that is great. If not, make it mandatory for each shift that starts. This way the bathrooms will not be forgotten and they will be cleaned three or four times a day.

Throughout this book you read examples of how treating your employees right assists in giving better customer service. They also need facilities that are clean, sanitary, and show that management is committed to their needs. Keeping this area to the standards you set on the sales floor will go a long way in promoting an employee friendly environment.

Now I do not expect all of you to run out and clean the bathroom locations at your business. But I do expect a better awareness of the bathrooms and how they are another tool for keeping the customers happy. It's one of many parts that make up the whole package.

- **Bathrooms should be clean, clean, clean!**
- **Make them a daily priority.**
- **Employee facilities are equally as important.**
- **Food services should be especially conscious.**

Seventeen

Hiring... Investing in the Future

"The art of progress is to preserve order amid change and to preserve change amid order."

—Alfred North Whitehead

Before my sixteenth birthday, I held down more than twenty different jobs. These included selling seeds, Christmas cards, cutlery door to door (I can still cut a penny with a pair of scissors) and many other interesting assignments. It seemed there was no job that did not interest me. The hiring process at this early stage in my life was a simple one. If you answered a few questions correctly, you were in.

During the college break, one of my best friends and I decided it might be a good idea if we went out and got a job for the summer. An ad in the local paper said a company was looking for one good laborer, and the ability to travel to California would be one of the requirements. For two guys from the flatlands of Illinois, this seemed like the perfect job! My friend and I went to the company and filled out an application. As we were waiting for the interview he looked over to me and said "You do realize only one of us is going to get the job." That is all it took. My competitive pride started taking over and all of a sudden one of my best friends next to me was now the enemy. I was no longer nervous about the interview but rather the fact of having to endure an entire summer of jesting from my friend if he got the job.

We were finally called into the room one at a time for the much anticipated interview session. I was sure he would ask me my grades, what other kinds of jobs I had previously, maybe even my construction experience which was zero at the time. Much to my dismay not one of those questions came up.

He had to leave the room for a minute to attend to some business in the shop when the phone started ringing. After listening to that obnoxiously loud ring for a few seconds I reached onto his desk and answered it. It was his brother who had just arrived from Florida and was meeting him for dinner that evening.

When the interviewer came back in I handed him a piece of paper with his brother's message. He seemed confused and startled by the mere fact that someone answered his phone and took a message without being told to do so. Throughout the remainder of the interview he asked what kind of hobbies I have, what's my favorite sports team, what size is my family and other questions that I was not quite sure why he was asking. The only thing I knew for sure was he still seemed bothered by the fact that somebody answered the phone.

A day later the phone rang and it was a nice woman telling me to report to work on Monday. I worked at this company for three summers until I finished college. At a work picnic I pulled the person who interviewed me over and asked why I got the job and my friend did not. He said it was simple and I remember his words still today. "We only hire enthusiastic people and ones that take charge of a situation without supervision." Later that night when his words really sank in, it became obvious the only advantage I had over my friend was that the phone in the office rang and I answered it.

One can pick up any newspaper today and find many more articles discussing firing than hiring. In the 1990s, the buzzwords among American corporations are downsizing and rightsizing. There are many contributing factors to these weight shedding measures but regardless, businesses today have committed themselves to make every hiring investment dollar count. Hiring the best today is not an advantage, but a necessity.

Whether your company is hiring a new president or a front-line sales clerk, the importance of determining what makes up the characteristics of your ideal employee will need to be understood. Finding the employee who works best in an organization will require an effort on your company's part greater than just filling out an application and saying we will call you later. The culture and environment already existing in your organization will set the tone for what type of talent you will be seeking in the hiring process. Companies committed to future growth take great pains to hire the right people.

Hiring the right people consists of determining what characteristics are needed to succeed in your business. If you are a video rental store, you will probably not be looking for someone who may fit in better at a jewelry store. That is, applicants must have a common trait that makes them ideal candidates for your business.

When hiring for a new front-line salesperson at my store, that person would have to go through a minimum of two interviews and oftentimes more. What organization has three hours to spend on conducting interviews for a salesclerk position? My answer is, what organization does not? Some of the best front-liners I ever worked with did not necessarily look good on paper. It was after the second or third interview that I would begin to tap into their potential in our environment.

I always tried to make it clear that our store was choosy about the people who were hired. The multiple interviews said we take longer than most of our competition because we take care of the people we hire and have a sincere interest in their growth. If you can make a future front-liner feel special before he or she is hired, you will discover a loyalty that is hard to come by in this day of continual turnover.

If I had a nickel for every time I saw an employee hired after only a fifteen minute interview, I would be on the retired golf circuit by now. First impressions are very important but we must remember judging is only part of the successful hiring equation. Analyzing the candidate, matching up the job role requirements, checking the references, and ensuring a good fit with the organization all are important pieces of the puzzle.

Team hiring is probably the best way to get the front-liners involved with the potential future hires. Many times management has a perception of what type of employee is needed for a particular area. The members of the team are experts on the qualifications needed by the applicant. They also understand existing demands and interpersonal styles that may indicate how well the new hire would fit in.

If interviewing for a cosmetic department position, I would have a cosmetician conduct one of the interviews. They tended to be better interviewers than I since they had a vested stake in that department. Since they would have to conduct the training, they wanted to ensure the chosen applicant would be around longer than three months. The other departments in the store worked similarly with some taking full responsibility for the entire hiring process.

On the new person's first day of work, make the event a celebration. If more than one new hire is starting, you may want to get the group together over some cookies and soda with a few of your key front-liners. They will not only begin to build a relationship with the other new employees but also a real sense of what type of culture exists in your organization. These new employee orientations can create enormous amounts of energy among the recruits. It was always refreshing to see the experienced front-liners encouraging the others and providing a comfort level even before their first Frontcounter™.

Attitudes and employee's approach to the job role far outweigh the technical background or skills they may bring with them. Let me give you an example.

A drugstore competitor nearby one of my earlier store locations went out of business with little notice. It was the end of the summer and many of the younger front-liners were going back to school and we found ourselves in a position to hire several new employees to fill the void. At the time this looked like a great opportunity to acquire some experienced drugstore people from the closed location. We could not have been more wrong!

At first it appeared to us that these new front-liners would be easy to train, highly productive, and bring us some new technical ideas that might be new to us. What we did not anticipate was the fact that although they had many years of drugstore experience, they did not understand the team concept. Quite honestly, we acquired a bunch of problems. The technical expertise they brought with them was far outweighed by their lack of performance and interpersonal skills.

When an organization takes the necessary time to do proper hiring, not only is it investing in it's own future but the customer's as well. Hiring the right front-liners is only the first step in giving great service. Providing proper training and fostering a winning service environment will ensure continued success.

I had a friend who did a lot of scouting for college football recruits. He would spend countless hours trying to find the exact recruit who would fit into his team. He knew the importance of finding the right candidates and took the time to make sure he got them.

The customers are having Frontcounters™ with newly hired employees that meet the criteria you set in the hiring process. There is a better chance they have the same characteristics as many of the front-liners you currently have working, thus share in the same commitment needed to be the best. These new front-liners catch on more quickly, give better service and last longer than those not properly hired.

When customers are unable to notice a decline in great service even when there are some new front-liners servicing their needs, than you can be assured you probably hired the right candidates. Like a farmer planting seeds early in the season, you will find out the time invested up front will produce a bountiful harvest.

So the next time you hire somebody and don't want to commit the time needed to do so, remember how long it takes to get rid of them!

- **Make every effort to hire the best front-liners that meet your criteria.**
- **Take the time up front to conduct extensive interviews.**
- **When hired, immediately make them feel like part of the team.**
- **Allow the new hires to partner with "buddies" to show them the ropes.**

Eighteen

Good vs. Great Service: Bridging the Gap

"The greatest pleasure in life is doing what people say you cannot
do."

−Chinese proverb

There's a saying that goes, "Do not burn the bridge
unless you are a great swimmer." We can all learn
something from these choice words.

Most businesses operating today do so under intense
competition. If you are one of the few that has no
competition, then you do not need to be a great swimmer to
survive. However, the rest of us better be providing great
service to avoid this pitfall.

The customers who increasingly shop stores today, have
a better chance to experience **average** customer service
versus **great** customer service. There is a huge gap between

the two and the businesses that are able to bridge this gap will be around for a long time to come.

Someone once asked me what are the obvious differences between the two. I explained it to him this way. It is the difference between Little League baseball and Major League. A cub and a lion. A Ford Escort and a Porsche. Are you beginning to see the differences?

In the service industry, the signs are just as obvious. Good or average customer service follows the more traditional approach of management. It is reactive rather than proactive. Putting out fires and solving problems after the fact are characteristics of this style of management. Most of the store team follows these types of expected service standards. The customers' expectations are rarely exceeded in this type of environment.

This customer service revolves around a policies and procedures type attitude. Customer complaints are viewed as failures and thus are not solicited. The employees have a laissez faire attitude regarding service above that which is exhibited by others in the store.

These types of conditions exist in too many of the businesses we go into every day. It is the "we will get by if we manage the problems as they come" attitude. As consumers expectations begin to rise, this level of service will not be tolerated. In fact if a competing business is smart, they will instantly recognize this weakness and take advantage of it.

Great service on the other hand requires an entire team effort. As I mentioned earlier there is a huge gap between good and great service. The bridge covering that gap is being built each day. Just as a construction crew must build a bridge one section at a time, the same is true of great service.

In the navy, by the time they finish painting the larger ships, it is time to start at the beginning again. Great service resembles this perpetual task, in that it must constantly strive each day to get a little further.

Once your business recognizes that providing average service will not differentiate you from most of the others out there, then you can begin isolating the factors that put your business on the same playing field as the great ones. It is at that point that we start walking up the ladder of success!

You know what great service represents. It's those few times that you leave a store or have a Frontcounter™ that is truly memorable. The kind that keeps you going back and back. For me, it is a little extra effort that shows the organization is committed to excelling in an area where many others have failed.

We have all read and heard about the Nordstroms, Wal-Marts, McDonalds and other businesses that are the best in giving great service. These companies deserve all the praise they receive for the consistent level of great service they demonstrate. They are pioneers and set the standards others must achieve if they want to be in this class of excellence.

After studying what separated these companies from others, I began to ask myself several questions. With the millions of businesses operating today, why do only a handful deliver great service? If so few companies are offering this type of service, is there a reason? Do they fully understand the rewards of providing great service?

The most similar trait among the elite service providers is the consistent reinforcement of accepting nothing less than the best service the front-liners can provide. This attitude serves as a continual reminder throughout the organization at all levels. This trait is not visible in the businesses that provide service at the average level, nor can it be taught without the organization completely redefining its service goals.

Teamwork is another visible characteristic of those industry leaders who truly define great service. It is instilled in the employees from the day they start. It is an effort from all who play a role in the delivering of great service.

The companies just mentioned have mastered this concept and work on perfecting it each and every day. Just as a great ballplayer must constantly stay tuned on the fundamentals of the game, the same is true of those who perform at an upper level of superior service.

The bridge I spoke about earlier not only separates these two groups, but magnifies the similarities of those who provide great service within an organization. The game is not to reinvent the wheel. It is to improve upon what others have taught us and make it fit within our business plan.

A close friend of mine is the master at performing this art. She will take all the information and experiences of others within her industry and bundle them into a neat little package that works at her store. In essence, she is providing the most complete package that is available to her and as a result, the organization reaps the huge dividends that come as a result of her not-so-creative thinking.

Chances are in your business there are hundreds of things you do right each day. That is great! But to be the best, this constant attempt at superior service must remain a top priority day in and day out. The slightest letdown will set your business back to the level of mediocrity.

If you are not sure where your organization ranks on the bridge to greatness, try this little test. Mentally picture a huge bridge connecting two islands. One end represents average service and the other side is great service. Where does your business fall on the bridge? Are you in the middle? Not far from the average side?

Each and every day you should monitor your progress across this bridge. Winning Frontcounters™, practicing good listening skills and the lessons mentioned in this book will all combine to help you get to the other side.

- **Bridging the gap to great customer service can be measured one day at a time.**
- **The difference between good and great service is no less than that between a rock and a mountain.**
- **Join the service leaders by providing great service at every available chance.**

Nineteen

Delivering Convenient Service

"Business is like a bicycle. Either you keep moving or you fall down."

—John David Wright

In today's hectic, fast-paced times, convenience and quick service have become a necessity. Those who are able to provide quick service when the customer demands it will have a greater opportunity of increasing their marks in the minds of the consumer. Those delivering slow, inefficient service, will find themselves trailing far behind the competition.

In the grocery business, the after work crowd represents an enormous dollar potential that if not handled properly will go elsewhere. At one of our Jewel/Osco stores in the western suburbs of Chicago, they advertise that all registers will be open from 4p.m. to 7p.m.. By this we are telling our customers that we understand the importance of getting you in and out as quickly as possible. After being at work all day, the last thing you want to do is stand in line at the grocery store for a gallon of milk.

The most visible aspect of the shopping experience for this customer is the checkout. It needs to be staffed with well-trained, knowledgeable, and friendly front-liners. Having checker training sessions during this crucial time is certainly not in the best interest of the customer. Staffing the checkouts requires the same management commitment that we devote to other areas of the store.

Recently, I stopped at one of our stores to pick up some allergy medicine for my wife after work. When I arrived at the checkout, there were ten people standing in line at one of the registers while another clerk was standing at her register with a puzzled look on her face.

I asked her if she was going to open up her register and she replied "I cannot, my drawer is $2 short." Embarrassed that this was one of our stores and ten people were waiting in line to checkout their purchases, I offered the clerk $2 to balance her drawer. She was stunned by this offer but refused and began recounting her drawer.

The manager came by and asked her what the problem was. She explained to him in front of the now growing number of customers that her drawer was short and she could not understand why. He told her to count the drawer again and let him know if it came out correctly. Even after noticing all the upset customers waiting in line, he walked away.

I could not believe the dismal display of service that I had just witnessed! Remember, this was one of our stores.

At a minimum he could have figured out why the drawer was $2 short after she had rung out the customers or at least bagged for the other checker who now had sixteen customers in her line. No, instead he fled to the safety of the office.

I immediately stormed up to the office to drag this manager by his ears if need be down to the checkout. He seemed startled by my presence and asked who I was. "A pissed off customer," I responded. Shocked that a total stranger was this upset at his poor service, he went downstairs and abruptly told the cashier not to worry about the shortage in the drawer and to open up her register. The group of customers, who were all very angry at this point, began clapping loudly. I wish you could have seen the look on that manager's face.

My goal was not to embarrass anybody, but I also knew that the owners of the company would not appreciate this poor display of service. If you see anybody including management giving poor customer service in your business, by all means let them know this is unacceptable. If it continues, let the district manager, vice-president or even the president know. Chances are, this behavior will not be tolerated.

Part of the magic equation is convenience. As just illustrated, that means getting them checked out as quickly as possible. Another key ingredient is ensuring the customers are able to find what they need easily. The store should be designed in such a fashion that the customer is danced through the different departments, not dragged. Coming to the store for a loaf of bread or a pair of running shoes should not involve investigative work.

A friend of mine tells an amusing story of the time he went to a major department store to purchase a wallet. After scouring the men's department unsuccessfully, he approached a male clerk who was straightening some clothes racks. The clerk did not know and asked a female assistant if she knew where the wallets were. She responded, "Oh yes" and told my friend to come with her.

As they headed into the maternity section, he thought maybe she did not understand exactly what he was looking for. A few steps later, there it was. A floor display of men's wallets. He could not help but ask the assistant why the wallets were in the maternity section. She was not sure herself but stated he was the second person she helped to find them.

Most stores are not this poorly merchandised but many pose great inconveniences to the customers if they are not able to find the products they are looking for. Keep it simple and logical to avoid any unnecessary frustrations for your customers.

If you offer sale circulars, these should be posted near the entrance before the customer begins his or her shopping. It is a simple gesture but one that will lead to better customer relations and increased sales. It is not magic.

Returns and exchanges are a part of many businesses. If these procedures are not taking place at the registers or if the store does them in a separate location, then identify them with a big, bold sign or banner. It's often frustrating to go into a store and track somebody down to find out where returns are done. It is also best to have these service desk or return areas near the front of the store so you do not further inconvenience an angry customer whose new roller blades just fell apart.

Hours of operation should be dictated by the customer's needs. My favorite dry cleaner stays open until 7p.m. during the week because it's convenient for her customers. Many of our stores are now open 24 hours a day because that is what the customer demands in our business. Video stores, banks, cafes – are all extending or rearranging their hours to better match these needs.

Offering convenience to customers requires listening to their desires and positively reacting to what they are telling you. Take a good look at your business and decide if there are any opportunities to provide better service through convenience type applications. Convenience + great service = loyal customers.

- **Cater to the customer's needs.**
- **Strive for new ways to offer greater convenience.**
- **Poor customer service is unacceptable at any level.**

Twenty

Mastering the Calm During the Storm

"A leader is best
When people barely know he exists,...
When his work is done, his aim fulfilled,
They will say: 'We did it ourselves'."

−Lao-Tz

Without question, it was one of the best NBA basketball contests I have ever seen. It was the final game of the first round playoffs that would send the winner into the second round to face the New York Knicks. My beloved Chicago Bulls and the Cleveland Cavaliers was the match-up in Richfield, Ohio.

Chicago was down one point with three seconds left to go in the game. The Chicago coach called a time-out and drew up the play that would give the Bulls a chance to win the game.

The entire stadium knew who was going to take the final shot. It would be number 23 − Michael Jordan. With thousands of fans booing and screaming for him to miss the shot, Michael sank it over a stretched out Cleveland Cavalier Craig Ehlo to win the game 101-100.

Remaining calm while the entire stadium was rooting against him helped Michael Jordan prepare mentally and emotionally. He was able to block out the distractions around him and concentrate on the objective at hand. Making the winning shot.

For the front-liner, it is equally important to remain calm when the storm comes. Not only will it better allow the front-liner to solve the customer's problem, but will also convey to the customer that the front-liner is confident in his or her ability to handle the situation.

Remaining in control with an angry customer is as simple as five easy steps. Master these and you will find yourself turning angry customers into satisfied ones.

1. **Relax.** Remember, the customer is probably angry at the organization or a particular area of the business that did not meet his or her needs. For the most part, it is not personal. Those fans in Cleveland did not dislike Michael Jordan as a person. Rather they were rooting for their team to win the game. Just as Michael remained calm during those final seconds in the game, you should keep relaxed and focused on the customer's needs.

2. **Listen.** Give the customers a chance to explain their concern. Not only will this give them an opportunity to vent their anger, they will probably begin to feel better getting the problem off their chests. Listening to the customer will allow you to fully understand what the severity of the problem might be. This means not interrupting and letting the customer finish explaining the problem in its entirety.

When he or she is finished talking, yelling, or screaming, then you can begin to win the customer back.

3. **Be compassionate.** As a customer explains a problem to you, do not roll your eyes or shake your head. This will only further upset the customer. Understand why they are upset and let them know you are equally concerned. When the customers notice that you care about their problems, they will begin to trust that you can solve their concern.

4. **Fix the customer.** Getting the customers back on your side requires immediate solutions to their problems. If you are out of an item on sale, do not just offer them a raincheck. Substitute a similar or better product even if it means you lose money on the item. Have the customer leave the store knowing that their concern was fixed.

5. **Correct the problem.** After you have won the customer back, investigate the problem and take appropriate measures to ensure it does not happen again. If a customer was angry the first time he or she came in, imagine his or her response a week later if the problem occurs again.

I have found these five simple steps will be your best weapons in the fight to keep your once angry customer coming back. There is great satisfaction watching an angry customer leave your store smiling after their problem has been fixed. As we learned in a prior chapter, this customer, if handled properly will become more loyal than before.

When my wife and I were expecting our first child, we attended some Lamaze classes to prepare for the special event. One of the concepts taught at the class was a breathing technique. I have found enormous benefits from this new-found tool to reduce stress. Taking deep breaths and exhaling can provide a relaxing effect. Whether you are stuck in traffic or just finished dealing with an angry customer, these few controlled breaths will put you at ease.

If you are in the service, retail, or restaurant business, on occasion you will be faced with upset customers. Properly handling of these customers can be accomplished by solving their problems and ensuring they do not happen again. Just as an NBA game has an audience, so do you as the other customers watch how you handle the angry one. Follow these five simple rules and you will also sink the winning shot.

* **Mastering the calm during the storm will be easier when you practice the rules above.**
* **Fix the customer and then fix the problem.**
* **Relaxing will benefit both you and the customer.**

Twenty-One
Customer loyalty

"Soon after the completion of Disney World someone said, 'Isn't it too bad Walt Disney didn't live to see this?' I replied, 'He did see it- that's why it's here.' "

—Mike Vance, Creative Director
Walt Disney Studios

Customer loyalty is one of the hottest topics in marketing today. Businesses are just stepping into these uncharted waters of understanding customer retention. Statistics have consistently shown that it is up to five times less expensive to sell to an existing customer than a new one. That being the case, it becomes apparent who is generating the profits. The loyal customers.

Loyalty marketing schemes have paved the way to enormous profits for those able to convert existing customers into loyal ones. Better yet, loyalty marketing has given some companies an unprecedented opportunity to attract new customers in the hopes of keeping them loyal for years to come.

Recently many in the automobile industry offered car buyers the chance to lease, thus postponing any decision to purchase outright. This allowed the car manufacturers to keep tabs on their new customers and establish a potential future relationship as well. Many marketing initiatives have followed in recent years. These include 30-day exchange programs, branded credit cards, free maintenance inspections and discounts, along with many others. Having a superior armory of loyalty weapons will prove itself as another tool in keeping satisfied customers returning.

Tom's of Maine listened to its brand loyal customers after a product reformulation caused many of them to become dissatisfied. Tom's reformulated its deodorants and anti-perspirants, which resulted in complaints from approximately half of the loyal users. Deciding against the risk of losing these loyal customers, Tom's opted for a $375,000 recall and switched back to the original formula. To its loyal customers, Tom's sent out a letter of explanation and a high value coupon to those who took the time to complain.

If there is a king of marketing product loyalty to their customers, the unanimous winner would be General Motors Corporation's Saturn subsidiary. They are the best at fostering a closer relationship between their customers and the company. The industry lingo for this is *relationship marketing* and it's one of today's hottest marketing buzzwords.

Each year, thousands of Saturn owners converge on the car company's headquarters in Spring Hill, Tennessee. Once there, the Saturn owners are treated to a three-day party and plant tour. Saturn is developing a long-term relationship while making its customers feel good about their purchase and bringing them back to do more business.

Saturn is attempting to convert potential one-time purchasers into long-term customers. By turning these relationships into partnerships, Saturn is building a brand loyal and potentially more rewarding customer.

Motorcycle maker Harley-Davidson, Inc. has catered to its loyal customers for years. By identifying its almost cult following, Harley-Davidson is getting the most out of this loyal relationship. It has an owners' club with more than 200,000 members and a 68 percent annual membership renewal.

Tom's of Maine, Saturn, and Harley-Davidson all understand the importance of loyal customers. All three sell more than just a product. Retaining their existing customers is their first priority. Making them loyal is second. After that and only after that, can attention be paid to the search for new customers.

Customer feedback is a crucial tool in servicing the needs of your loyal customers. This program must be managed to the same degree as a winning sales strategy–often and in dollar terms. Satisfaction is a precondition of loyalty, but may not be a predictor. To predict customer loyalty, you must measure key indicators such as their intention to purchase your products in the future.

Conventional wisdom has shown that higher quality brings higher customer satisfaction. Be careful! Higher customer satisfaction does not always result in customer loyalty. This is the key flaw in customer satisfaction measurement. Actual customer behavior is a much better gauge when soliciting customer feedback. Quality is about what customers do, not what they say.

Based on the statistics of what the average family spends on groceries in a given lifetime, a customer that shops a single store has revenue potential of $284,000. It still amazes me how business would ever jeopardize this group of devoted shoppers through improper complaint handling or not listening to their needs. Although we will discuss complaint handling in the next chapter, let's take a look how it affects your loyal customer.

When they become dissatisfied with a negative experience with your organization, will they defect to competition and quit patronizing your business altogether? When soliciting their feedback, you must measure the degree to which negative experiences result in the customers defecting. The best way to prevent these longtime customers from leaving is to encourage their complaints and make sure they are corrected immediately. This group of loyal customers expects not just to be heard but reacted to.

By encouraging your customers to complain, you can raise their loyalty as much as 50 percent when you satisfy their needs. Your least loyal customers are the ones who do not complain. The trick is to get this group to be more vocal and strive to delight them with your quick response. This is an opportunity to turn a shopper into a customer. Then you can work on turning this customer into a partner.

Another tool for identifying your customers is customer loyalty programs. These programs work best when built up over time when a relationship is developed with the customer.

Smart cards, preferred cards, and frequent shopper cards are a few of the many names attached to business

loyalty programs operating today. Point collection or discounts are designed to keep the customer coming back time and again. Competitive pressure has forced companies to search for profit growth within an unexploited customer base. With increased technology, these cards offer the business more database marketing opportunities.

The most visible loyalty program operating today is the Discover Card with its cash back program. They entice customers to use their card in order to get a rebate at the end of the year based on their purchases. These cards and programs have shown amazing results in increased loyalty and customer retention. Not only does the business learn more about the customer and his or her shopping pattern, but it will also maintain a higher retention rate through the use of these programs.

One more tool for your loyalty arsenal is making the customer feel special. Treat them as if they are VIPs each and every visit. With a smart card program, you will be able to identify this group and cater to its sometimes complex needs.

Casinos often indulge their biggest players. They will drive them to the airport in a limousine, put them on an airplane, bring them to the hotel for a few days, and provide special services that only a VIP would receive. The casinos know who their best customers are and treat this group like royalty.

Businesses can learn a valuable lesson from this. What if they treated their loyal customers in a fashion that left them feeling special? Do you think they would return time and time again? I do.

When I do business with an organization and it strives to make me feel special, there is a better chance that I will remain loyal. From the dry cleaners down the street to the bakery we visit most Saturday mornings, they make us feel valued each and every time we use them. They know the key to a successful future is making their present day customers know they are important.

In a time when superstores and warehouse businesses are offering rock bottom prices, it becomes increasingly difficult to compete. If your business can understand the economics of loyal customers and the financial gain of keeping them, then you will compete in an arena that few have mastered.

- **Customer loyalty brings increased market share through repeat sales and referrals.**
- **Customer loyalty reduces costs of doing business.**
- **Customer loyalty creates a partnership between customer and business.**
- **Loyal customers have proven to generate the most profits.**

Twenty-Two

Ca$hing in
on Complaint$

"There's no off-season anymore."

—Nolan Ryan

While shopping for a birthday present for my wife, I noticed that the store had a unique sign posted near the register. It said, "Complaints are only wanted after the store is closed." Now as a potential buyer of goods in this store, what motivation do I have to offer a complaint if I felt one was needed. This store is not interested in hearing from the customers. It is unfortunate because a customer that feels their concerns are not listened to will go elsewhere.

Across the country, front-liners are dealing with customers who have experienced a product or service failure. How they respond to these customers can very often turn disappointment into customer satisfaction. The first step is teaching the front-liners that complaints represent a positive chance to win back the customer.

Research has shown that a customer who has a problem corrected ends up more loyal than a customer who has never had a problem. These consumers identify organizations that listen to their concerns and than fix them. When this happens, the customers know if in the future they experience a problem, they can be assured it will be corrected.

Sometimes problems are unavoidable. One way to ensure a disappointed customer's business is not lost is to encourage buyers to report any complaints immediately. Let them know that if they are not happy, you want to know about it.

A neighborhood grocery store in the Lincoln Park area of Chicago has a bulletin board mounted near the exit of the store. Posted on the board are some customer comment cards and complaints with regard to a wide range of issues. Attached to each of these cards is a response from a manager or department head describing what will be done to correct the problem.

By posting these cards, this store is letting its customers know that complaints are welcome. Those shoppers who had no complaints at the store are assured that any future concerns will be addressed. Being dependent on a neighborhood customer base allows this business no room to lose even one customer.

Since the time most of us were little children, our parents told us "Quit complaining." Complaining was not something you were encouraged to do. More often, if you did complain, there was a good chance discipline or punishment would soon follow.

Today, management comes along and attempts to teach the team and customers that complaints are not bad. However, a trait that has been instilled in the front-liners since a very early age cannot be dramatically changed with a few choice sentences. Just as with most things in life, actions speak louder than words.

Show them the financial damage of even one customer lost due to poor complaint handling. Let them see how you handle a complaint and how quickly the customer is identified. Train the front-liners to be specialists who have the education and work experience to develop problem solving and communication skills.

After you have instituted a complaint handling program for the employees, it is at that point that your business can begin to educate the customers to voice their concerns. Businesses should make it easy for customers to voice their dissatisfaction by establishing a complaint handling system. Satisfying complaints begins with receiving them. Although there are numerous way to accomplish this, these represent a sure-fire way of getting positive results.

1. Empower all front-liners to be customer service specialists. Or, designate a customer service executive properly trained to drive the program.

2. Make available customer comment cards that leave plenty of room for their individual concerns. They should be short, simple to read, and be reacted to immediately.

3. One of the easiest ways to encourage a customer to complain is to provide an 800 number. Establishing an 800 number for customer questions and concerns will prove a competitive advantage. Staff it with properly trained personnel and this department will pay for itself.

4. Record all complaints in a master log. After they are recorded, identify if there is a particular area that needs improvement.

5. Track results! CEOs and executives show a real commitment to the organization in handling customer complaints, when results are tracked and measures are put in place to correct shortcomings.

Statistics show that more than 70 percent of people do not complain about a product or service. That leaves only 30 percent of upset customers that your business has a chance to help with a positive complaint response. For the business that is customer driven, a motivated store team knowledgeable in complaint handling is your best weapon.

With this in place, the front-liners now understand that proper complaint handling represents a positive chance to win back the customer. In turn, the customers are encouraged to participate in the program. Now let's look at some of the characteristics of the front-line service specialists and how they affect the complaint handling program.

A good customer service specialist understands a positive opportunity exists and is prepared not only to listen but to hear what the complainer has to say. A key to this is understanding what the customer expected to receive and what the customer actually did receive. In all too many cases, a set of expectations regarding a product or service falls short, leaving the customer feeling cheated.

A customer service specialist can often identify when a customer is upset or does not complain directly. Sometimes these customers need a little prompting or encouragement to find out what has disappointed them. Recognizing who these consumers are can often result in fixing a potential problem before they leave the store.

Speaking of fixing, those companies that run the best complaint management programs have shown increased profits yearly. They have found the true cost or benefit of complaints can be calculated by the gross benefits of effectively handled complaints divided by the costs of running a complaint program. Of the businesses I have studied, all have turned this into a money making unit.

Organizations selling to consumers win most of the accolades for the best complaint handling systems. But smart business-to-business firms are not lagging very far behind. They too are beginning to establish relationships with vendors, suppliers and others who make an impact on their business.

Complaint handling combines all the skills we learned so far in this book and molds them into a positive package. Empowerment, word-of-mouth (the eleven or twelve other people they will tell about their poor experience), bending rules, and many more give the front-liner the edge needed to satisfy the customers who were disappointed.

All businesses have complaints and react to them in different ways. Offer your customers an environment where complaints are welcomed and encourage them as often as necessary. Those that are customer driven will ca$h in on an effective complaint handling program.

- Recognizing then satisfying complaints represents a competitive advantage.
- Satisfying complaints begins with receiving them.
- Complaint handling units can be a profitable activity.
- Train and staff the business with those who have developed problem-solving and communication skills.

Twenty-Three
I Guarantee It

The will to win is important, but the will to prepare is vital.
                                                  —Joe Paterno

Nordstrom does it. Lands' End does it. Eddie Bauer, Stew Leonard and L.L. Bean all do it. What do these leaders in customer satisfaction have in common? They all offer unconditional, no questions asked guarantees. If you are not happy with something you have purchased, they will take it back for any imaginable reason.

Why? It's simple. They want your business. The legendary stories of Nordstrom and Stew Leonard circulate around the world every day. Most of you by now have heard the folklore surrounding these service giants. If not, here are two stories to whet your appetite to start your own guarantee program.

The story goes that an angry customer came into Nordstrom's complaining about a set of automobile tires she had purchased at the store but was not satisfied with. The customer service representative at the store asked the customer to simply bring the tires in and her account would be credited in full. This despite the fact that Nordstrom does not even carry tires.

Stew Leonard's in Norwalk, Connecticut, is America's best-known supermarket. A customer came into the store to return a melon she claimed to have purchased at the store. Without question, Leonard took the melon and gave the customer her money back even though his store did not carry that particular melon. Why? Leonard says he would not let $50,000 worth of business walk out the door because of a "lousy melon." That is one of the many reasons why the store was listed in the *Guinness Book of World Records* for doing more business per square foot than any other store in the entire world.

The customers are always right. Wrong! The customers are not always right but they always win. In the two examples above, the customers were incorrect about where they purchased the goods. However, they won because the businesses value their future spending power and want them coming back. I taught my employees that the customer is not always right but when they leave, they better think they are. The saying goes, "A winner never makes a loser feel like one." When satisfying customers' concern, it is important to make them winners each and every time.

To be effective, a guarantee has to be exciting. This guarantee should promise exceptional, uncompromising quality, and back that promise with compensation to fully recapture the customers good will. Hotels, supermarkets,

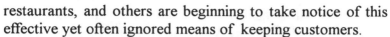

restaurants, and others are beginning to take notice of this effective yet often ignored means of keeping customers.

Hampton Inns found that offering a full refund to its customers was effective. Although it paid out $1.1 million in 1993 to dissatisfied customers, it estimates that the guarantee brought in $11 million of additional revenue.

Hampton offers a 100 percent Satisfaction Guarantee promising high quality accommodations, friendly efficient service and comfortable surroundings. Having stayed at their inns on several occasions, I can attest to this promise of great service.

The real value of offering a guarantee is not simply as a marketing tool, but rather as a method of focusing the organization and driving performance. For a company committed to delivering on its promises, a guarantee will help it focus on its customers. Customer satisfaction is delivered by being very explicit about what your business will deliver and then adhering to those policies. It keeps us on our toes each day when the business is driven by a guarantee to satisfy its customers. An organization that fails to honor its guarantee is worse off than an organization having no guarantee at all.

A guarantee instills a sense of confidence in the consumers who shop your stores. Whether a guarantee program will be the centerpiece of your organization or simply a promotional tool, it offers the customers an opportunity that others in your industry may not.

Unfortunately, many organizations hesitate to guarantee their products and services for fear that customers will take advantage of them. Although a few individuals may purposely attempt to take benefit from this, it still makes good business sense to offer a guarantee.

One of my favorite books is *The Old Country Store*. It tells tales dating back to 1791. One such story is about a man who wanted to buy $50 worth of goods, a nice order, but said he hesitated to buy because he had been swindled by the merchants he had dealt with in the past. The dealer said he would fill the order on a money-back-if-not-satisfied basis. He put up the order, and wrote across the bottom of the bill, "Your money back if you want it" and signed his name. Later the customer came in and asked for his money back.

"What's the matter, weren't the goods all right?" asked the merchant.

"No they weren't," said the man.

"All right, bring them back," said the retailer, and thought he had him there. The customer pointed to his receipted bill.

"It doesn't say anything there about having to bring the goods in."

I tell you this tale to demonstrate that some individuals will always test your policy. Even though this episode took place more than a hundred years ago, the country merchant knew the importance of offering a guarantee and some of the minor irritations that come along with it.

On a plane headed to Salt Lake City, Utah this year, I sat next to a sales rep who sold outdoor boat motors. He was very excited about a presentation he was going to make about their new line of motors. I asked the fellow how business was in that industry since I was not very familiar with it. He stated it was just average until they offered a three month guarantee on all their outboard motors. Now, it has become difficult to keep up with the demand.

When asked why this guarantee was so important, he responded, "They were the first in the industry to offer such a guarantee." Their line was slightly more expensive than some of the other motors and most consumers could not afford to take a chance. Now with this new promise of satisfaction, people were willing upgrade to a more expensive motor with the understanding of complete satisfaction.

A properly instituted guarantee program will add new life and opportunities for your business. Let the customers know you stand behind the goods and services your business offers. Let all who visit know they are to be completely satisfied or you will make it right. It will give added lift to your customer service program. I guarantee it!

- **Guarantees are not a losing program. If monitored, they offer additional revenue and customers.**
- **Be the first in your industry to offer a guarantee.**
- **Honor all requests no matter how unusual.**
- **Guarantee programs yield greater confidence in your services and products.**

Twenty-Four

Service Superstars
That Make a Difference

"What counts is the not necessarily the size of the dog in the fight-it's the size of the fight in the dog."

—Dwight D. Eisenhower

A s you have seen, I love to tell stories that illustrate and teach life's little service lessons. Some are excellent examples of how organizations are committed to providing the service environment that works. Others, perhaps the majority, struggle at customer service from every available angle. A small minority are so pathetic in their attempt at service that it boggles the mind how they have stayed in business to this point.

Outlining all the different pieces that were to be a part of this book, I knew that this type of chapter would have to be included for one important reason. It is my chance to say thank you to those who exhibited the kind of service that most businesses dream about. These businesses and front-liners left lasting impressions with me of how they viewed service and the importance it played within their stores.

Now so people don't accuse me of being biased, I have not included the food/drug retailing industry. I believe American Stores provides one of the best service stores across the country. It's our No. 1 priority and we do it better than most. Although many examples of great and poor service have been provided within our industry, it would not be appropriate to write about these without being judged fairly.

Let's journey now to the stores and businesses that have left such a positive impact that they are featured here. All are true Frontcounters™ that contain one important concept. The delivery of great service. Here we go!

 Sheila Buralli - Marshall Field's

I was in the Marshall Field's store on State Street in Chicago trying on shoes one Sunday afternoon. I explained to the salesman that I wear orthopedic inserts and that I would need an extra wide shoe. After bringing me the shoes that I asked for and inserting the insoles, he proceeded to put a metal shoehorn inside the shoe and ripped the insoles. At $350 a pair, needless to say I was not very happy.

After I explained to him what he had just done, he apologized and gave me the name of the person I could contact to have the insoles replaced. The next morning, I called the name on the card which was Sheila Buralli. She works in the Human Resource Department at Marshall Field's and listened to my problem with much concern.

Soon after this conversation, Sheila contacted my podiatrist who made new insoles at no charge to me. She apologized for the inconvenience and thanked me for calling her.

No hassles, polite service and quick action all made this potentially problematic situation a great experience. Sheila was more concerned with losing a customer and exceeded my expectations. Great job!

Millie Lutzow - Wendy's Old Fashioned Hamburgers in Loves Park, Illinois

If you are ever in the Rockford/Loves park area and want a great burger and a little scratch, there's only one place to go. Let me explain. After visiting some Osco Drug stores in the area, we stopped at Wendy's for a quick bite to eat. After sitting down with our meals, a mature front-liner who worked there approached us asking if we had our scratch yet today?

We were a little puzzled by the question but before we knew it, Millie was beginning to lightly scratch our backs. It only lasted a few seconds but made our day to see this kind of unique service You see, Millie is known for her scratches and she explained that although it's difficult to get to everybody, she tries to make sure at least her regulars get their daily scratchs.

The next time I get a little itch on my back that I'm not able to reach, maybe I'll drive up to Wendy's in Loves park and get a burger and a scratch.

 Roger Blinkel- Sydney, Australia

On the recommendation of many of the locals in Sydney, Pam and I took a bus tour to the Blue Ridge mountains of Australia. After arriving in a little city at the foot of the mountains, we did some shopping until the local bus came that would take us up. I guess you could say we did more shopping than we should have. We missed the bus and another one was not coming for quite a while.

That's when we met Roger. Roger drives the bus that goes within the city but not up to the mountains. That is, before he met my wife and me. Everything you may have heard about the friendliness of the Australian people is true .

After we explained our predicament to Roger, he ordered us to get in because he would take us up to the mountains. Along the way he picked up a regular who demanded of Roger that he take us via the scenic route. They conversed as if they were old friends and when we came upon one of the more beautiful ridges, he pulled the bus over and let us out. He said he would be back soon, after he dropped off the other passenger.

After Pam and I got out to take in the magnificent scenery, Roger drove off. About twenty minutes later he drove up and the three of us headed up to the Blue Ridge Mountains. I don't know about you, but when was the last time you had a bus driver give you this type of red carpet treatment?

Tricia - Ranalli's

Ranalli's is a very quaint Chicago pizza restaurant that is known for its delicious double decker pizza and extensive beer list. Besides ordering the above selections, we also ordered the calamari appetizer dish. Tricia was our waitress that evening. After she brought it to the table, we soon discovered that Ranalli's should stick to the pizza and beer. The calamari tasted awful and no one at the table would eat it.

Tricia noticed we had not partaken in the appetizer and asked us if we were not happy with it. We briefly told her it was not very good. She immediately took it off the table and assured us it would be taken off the bill. It seems that she had other customers who also had not particularly enjoyed the calamari. Tricia said she would alert management to the problem and apologized for the inconvenience.

After the meal, Tricia brought us the bill with a receipt that said " no charge". On it she wrote "Give us a try again soon." When I have colleagues who come to town and want great Chicago pizza, you can bet it is back to Ranalli's. No, not for the calamari. Instead for the pizza, beer, and caring service.

Kathy O'Donnell - United Airlines

Much of my job entails constant travel. If you have ever had to travel for a living, you know it can be a frustrating experience when your plane leaves late or not at all. Here is one person who made a difference to brighten up a tired traveler's day.

After meetings in Anaheim, California, I drove to the airport to get home for a close friend's birthday party. The day had consisted of long meetings without agreement on some important issues since the early morning hours. Normally I am a very jovial person; arriving at the airport gate, I was not in a very good mood.

Kathy, who was behind the counter, noticed this and asked me if I had a bad day. I told her, "Let's just say it was not a good one." She gave me back my ticket and I boarded the plane.

After stepping on the plane, I noticed the boarding pass had designated 2B as my seat. Kathy had put me in first class. A very simple gesture that made my day. Thanks, Kathy!

Marriott Residence Inn - Phoenix, Arizona

It's not much fun being away from home, but staying at this inn made it a little more enjoyable. Unlike many of the others I have stayed at on my numerous trips, this group offers an almost neighborly approach to customer satisfaction. They performed all the everyday services that they have become known for. But the whole group of front-liners there also treated their guests to a little extra special care.

Since business kept me traveling to Phoenix quite frequently, I was almost a regular here. They would greet me late at night when I came home. If it was a real late meeting, I would find breakfast (Cocoa Puffs and chocolate milk) at my door in the morning so I could get a few extra minutes of sleep. This superior effort didn't stop there.

When I checked in, they would greet me by name. They arranged to get me a temporary membership at a health club across the street. Shall I go on?

After deciding to spend a weekend in Phoenix, I arranged to have my wife come out and join me. When I returned from the airport with her, much to my surprise, there was a bottle of champagne and flowers in my room.

In the billion-dollar travel industry, competition for your dollar is intense It's this constant exceeding of expectations that keeps me going back when I'm in the Phoenix area.

O'Neil's- Winnetka, Illinois

Scott Krone, a good neighbor of mine, passes along this customer service victory. These are his words.

"I ordered a take out meal from O'Neil's. I had an evening meeting and had ordered the meal with the idea of eating at my parents' home.

As I got out of the car, my entire meal fell out of the bottom of the bag. The main sauce from the entree had leaked out of its packaging and disintegrated the bottom of the bag. The entree fell out of the packaging and onto the driveway. After I tried to salvage the meal, which was not possible, I discovered the sauce had spilled on my briefcase and on my car's upholstery.

I tried to clean both my briefcase and my car but was not too successful. I telephoned O'Neil's and explained the situation. The manager offered to replace my meal, but I did not have time to pick up a new dinner. She took my name and number and told me the owner would call me tomorrow.

At nine o'clock the next morning, Pat O'Neil called me. I explained the situation to him and told him about my briefcase and car. Pat's immediate response was he wanted to reimburse me for my dinner. I told him I was not concerned about the dinner, but rather the damages I incurred. I told him the briefcase was worth about $300, not to mention the cost to clean the car. Pat asked if it was possible to repair the briefcase, and offered to pay the expense. I said I would go to the store where I purchased the briefcase and ask.

The store told me that the sauce had permanently damaged the leather case and it could not be repaired. I asked the sales clerk what the retail value of the briefcase was. She said it was about $200.

I called Pat and explained to him what I had learned. He said he would write me a check for $200 and also to make sure that the next time I need to order food to call him. O'Neil's would pick up the cost for the dinner. As he explained, 'O'Neil's is in the business of pleasing people and wanted to show me that they could prepare a take out order correctly!'"

Pat O'Neil recognizes that each customer is important. He understands the risks of losing Scott as a customer and the possibility of many more through negative word-of-mouth.

USAA Emergency Road Service- San Antonio, Texas

If there was a modern day calvary, USAA would be it. This group of highly trained personnel delivers some of the best service available with one small exception. They usually deal with the customer after their vehicle has broken down.

My wife has had her fair share of mechanical breakdowns in recent years. Any time she needed towing, a jump start, or any other type of assistance, a phone call to USAA would have help soon on the way.

Any of the operators who take a stranded motorist's call, soon put that person at ease with their assurance of quick help. They are trained to deal with upset and often times angry customers. I know Pam has been impressed numerous times with their concern level and the professional handling that each call gets.

All of these individuals and organizations have earned my highest respect. Congratulations because you are truly the best.

Twenty-Five

The Fat Lady's About to Sing

"The choice is between doing something and doing nothing, and doing nothing never gets you anywhere."

—Felix G. Rohatyn

When I set out to write this book, I wanted to share some service lessons and ideas that might help an individual or organization reach a higher level of customer awareness. My goal was to provide these tales in a fun to read format that could be applied immediately. If this is not the case, I have failed.

In this book, we have witnessed individuals who strive to make every Frontcounter™ a rewarding one. They know the importance of giving great service and the satisfaction that comes from it. These front-liners are the unsung heroes all businesses should strive to have working on their side.

We also looked at some who have not provided customer service to our standards. Many of these people have failed at delivering customer satisfaction because the organization they work for has failed in providing a service first environment. They need leadership that allows them to correct problems instantaneously and make decisions with the customers'concerns a priority. All organizations are capable of changing to a customer driven business if the right attitude prevails and the front-liners are allowed to delight the customers.

The term Frontcounter™ was also introduced. This is the critical point that many customers base their future purchase decisions on. These important interactions are the day in and day out fundamental responsibilities of all organizations that maintain customer service as their highest priority. A business is well on its way to success when it learns to manage and identify these Frontcounters™.

Absent from this book were complicated graphs and charts that dissect the service industry but provide few applicable solutions for correcting the problems. We could read all the customer service books in the world, but they don't hold water if the front-liners do not understand them.

This book was dedicated to and written for the front-liners out there who care about the quality of service they deliver. Its intent was to reach those who shared similar experiences and frustrations. Whether you're serving an internal or external customer, it's all about *Winning at the Front-Line.*

Do you have a story to tell? Is there a lasting service experience that angered or delighted you? The author would like to hear your tales from the front-line. I hope to

include many of your stories and comments in my next book.

Please write to:

Foto Publishing
c/o Brian Dennis
635-5 Chicago Ave
Suite # 258
Southport Plaza
Evanston, IL
60202

Index